Visiting
Sexual
Exploitation

Visiting Sexual Exploitation

How Should Indonesia Strengthen Its Policies
to Curb Sex Work in Response to
Its Extramarital Sex Criminalization

JASON HUNG

ISEAS YUSOF ISHAK
INSTITUTE

First published in Singapore in 2024 by
ISEAS Publishing
30 Heng Mui Keng Terrace
Singapore 119614
E-mail: publish@iseas.edu.sg
Website: http://bookshop.iseas.edu.sg

The responsibility for facts and opinions in this publication rests exclusively with the author and his interpretations do not necessarily reflect the views or the policy of the publisher or its supporters.

ISEAS Library Cataloguing-in-Publication Data

Name(s): Hung, Jason, author.
Title: Visiting sexual exploitation : how should Indonesia strengthen its policies to curb sex work in response to its extramarital sex criminalization? / by Jason Hung.
Description: Singapore : ISEAS-Yusof Ishak Institute, 2024. | Includes bibliographical references and index.
Identifiers: ISBN 9789815104707 (soft cover) | 9789815104714 (ebook PDF) | 9789815104776 (epub)
Subjects: LCSH: Sex and law—Indonesia. | Adultery—Law and legislation—Indonesia. | Sex work—Government policy—Indonesia. | Indonesia—Social conditions.
Classification: LCC HV6593 I5H93

Cover design by Lee Meng Hui
Index compiled by Raffaie Nahar
Typeset by Superskill Graphics Pte Ltd
Printed in Singapore by Markono Print Media Pte Ltd

Contents

1

Introduction

ABSTRACT

In the introductory chapter, I introduce Indonesia's latest criminal code that criminalizes the act of extramarital sex. Then, I delineate the prevalence of commercial sex activities and indicate how prostitution is religiously, socially and legally prohibited and socially undesirable. (Riswanda, Nantes, and Mills 2016). Here I find the need to emphasize the exposure of the existing research gap on addressing commercial sex and sex tourism in contemporary Indonesia's sex trade market primarily or exclusively, as literature prefers examining organized sex crimes in Thailand, Cambodia or Southeast Asia in general (Davy 2014; Rojanapithayakorn 2006). I highlight the importance of addressing prostitution in Indonesia, as such activity, given the religious and historical contexts, is deemed highly controversial domestically. To conclude the chapter, I present the contents that will be discussed in the following chapters, as an overview of the focus of this book.

INTRODUCTION

On 13 April 2023, I returned to Taipei City, Taiwan, after spending the preceding months in Boston, Cambridge (United Kingdom), Kuala Lumpur and Bangkok. I was appointed as a visiting fellow at the Institute of Sociology, Academia Sinica in Taiwan and a fellow at Harvard University Asia Centre in Boston in 2022/23. As my research endeavours in Boston had already been wrapped up, I relocated to Taipei City to fulfil my research errands prior to the end of my visiting fellowship appointment contract (i.e., 30 June 2023). On 18 April 2023, I met my native Taiwanese friend who has been a typical digital nomad and usually spends her time in Tokyo, Taipei City and Europe. We were having a conversation over a few cups of ice-drip coffee. I told her I was recently working on a monograph on Indonesia's extramarital sex criminalization—the book that you are now reading. She was taken aback by the topic of my research investigation not only because she had not realized Indonesia has criminalized anti-extramarital sex, but more because she had never expected any Asian country of today would practise such a societally controversial and perhaps "morally outdated and/or conservative" law (note: In Chapter 5, I will explain why passing such a law is contextually important to Indonesia).

I was not surprised by her initial response, as I was equally shocked when I first heard Indonesia's parliament was passing a criminal code to criminalize extramarital sex. Here, a married adult can be jailed for one year for performing extramarital sex; while unmarried couples could face up to six months in jail if they cohabit (McCarthy 2022). I was a native Hong Kong Chinese who enjoyed the opportunity to receive higher education in the United Kingdom and conduct research projects on social inequality, sexual health and social policy examinations in the United States. One of the privileges of attending higher education in the United Kingdom is probably the "satisfactory" short term-times (i.e., some six to seven months per academic year). Especially when I am, as of writing this book, in my final year of PhD research at the University of Cambridge (given my completion of the doctoral thesis), I have been given the opportunities to flexibly manage my schedule throughout the year. You can always find me, on and off, spending half a year in the United Kingdom, another three months in the United States—for research—and the remaining three months in Southeast Asia for leisure.

In academia, there is a term called "leisure migration". Usually, the term is used to describe people migrating to socio-economically, and perhaps racially, less privileged regions to seek a better quality of life. Leisure migrants are common in Southeast Asia, in which Western men who are financially established, compared to average Southeast Asian standards, and racially privileged would migrate to, for example, sex tourist-popular or vacation-popular destinations to maintain a satisfactory quality of life while enjoying lower living costs. I am not trying to present myself as a leisure migrant, as I am, at most, a frequently travelled tourist who likes to be exposed to different cultures, linguistic heritage and communities. However, I would coin myself a "leisure tourist" who regularly spends my months off in Southeast Asia for relaxation and recharge.

Especially when I have never anticipated returning to my birthplace—Hong Kong—so spending my vacation months in different Southeast Asian countries has long been my interest. I, on and off, have been living in Thailand for over three years, a country that, despite my foreigner status, I would proudly call my second home. Prior to my residency in Thailand, I added up spending over six to seven months in the city of Jakarta in my early twenties. There I had known ample Indonesian natives, dated an Indonesian lady and encountered many, good or bad, cultural practices that were designated for Muslims. Most of my Indonesian friends are Muslims. They usually follow quite strict Islamic practices. For example, if Indonesian girls work for institutions in the public sector, they always wear hijabs when going to work. Also, Indonesian Muslims often comply with their religious beliefs and values, so they are prone to use Islamic concepts to justify or rationalize others' or their own behaviours. That being said, however, like in any other country, extramarital sex is low-key common in Indonesia. Such extramarital affairs include cheating on non-marital and marital partners and finding commercial sex when needed. From what I heard from my Indonesian ex-girlfriend and people from her social networks, quite a lot experienced extramarital affairs at some point in their lifetime. Some might even be actively but covertly seeking hookups or commercial sex. In addition, some might even work as freelance sex workers in order to earn extra financial resources while overtly spending their time as full-time students and/or employees.

When Indonesia's parliament announced that the country would criminalize anti-extramarital sex, many of my Indonesian friends were outrageous and frustrated, like the mass majority as reported on local, regional and international news outlets. We all know the elephant in the room. Regardless of whether we are affiliated with Christianity, Catholicism, Islam or else religions, or are atheists, we might be exposed to, higher or lower, risks of seeking non-marital sexual satisfaction. While such behaviour is religiously and morally condemned, as a sociologist, I cannot ignore the existence of such a social phenomenon. Only when we acknowledge the assumption that a proportion of us, regardless of religious affiliation, might ever experience non-marital sex, dissidents can justify why they have denounced the decision of Indonesia's parliament to criminalize extramarital sex as a violation of personal freedom.

It is not of interest to examine the reasonability for criminalizing those who ever have extramarital sex in Indonesia. I would like to take this opportunity to articulate the relationship between Indonesia's controversial legal policymaking output and the notorious Southeast Asian problem of prevailing commercial sex activities. In Indonesian society, sex is supposed to occur only within marriage. Women working in occupations that require engagement in extramarital sex, such as in the sex industry, significantly suffer from a damaged reputation and victimization of social and cultural stigmatization (Parker 2016). As of writing this book, two of my relevant monographs entitled *Breaking the Unequal Power Structure: A Discourse on Poverty-Led Crime in Southeast Asia* and *Legalising Prostitution in Thailand: A Policy-Oriented Examination of the (De-)Construction of Commercial Sex* are under peer-review by Palgrave Macmillan and Springer Nature respectively. The Palgrave Macmillan monograph spends a lengthy chapter section discussing how prostitution and sex trafficking in Indonesia are poverty driven. My Springer Nature monograph, alternatively, thoroughly discusses Thailand's recently proposed law of legalizing sex work and addresses what the drafted law, if passed, means to Thai, child or adult, prostitutes' rights, development, health and well-being. In this book, I would like to extend my area focus to Indonesian contexts, by delineating how prostitution has been socio-economically and institutionally constructed and by arguing how criminalizing anti-extramarital sex would mean to the prevalence of sex work, or vice versa. Only when we analyse how prostitution has been built or driven, we can better understand how to destruct the root causes of sex work and how to mitigate the barriers to preventing such a profession from being alleviated or eliminated.

This book, therefore, discusses the controversies and feasibility concerns imposed by Indonesia's recent criminalization of anti-extramarital sex. I address the nuances between Indonesian and Islamic values and/or norms, extramarital sex (including commercial sex) and the country's possible sustainable development. I also examine what the criminalization of extramarital sex means to Indonesia's tolerance of, and attitudes towards, underage or not, sex work. By disclosing how prostitution and related crimes (such as sex trafficking) are constructed, I am able to explore the problems of poverty, socio-economic disadvantages and institutional loopholes in Indonesian society. By problematizing the status quo of the structure of Indonesia and local governing agencies, I can deliver evidence-based policy recommendations to help alleviate, and even eradicate, the root causes of prostitution and sex trafficking in order to facilitate the crackdowns on the domestic sex industry. Here I, then, visit extramarital sex criminalization and declare how cracking down on the structure of sexual exploitation domestically helps Indonesia curb the prevalence of extramarital sex overall. The final chapter outlines how extramarital sex criminalization is contextually significant in Indonesia, despite such an act being deemed a human rights violation in non-Islamic settings. Given the contextual significance, I conclude that effectively, consistently and timely addressing the root causes of prostitution and sex trafficking helps shrink the sex trade market and, ultimately, the prevalence of extramarital affairs in Indonesia. This book, last but not least, details what individual-level, community-level and social-level benefits can be gained when Indonesia curbs the prevalence of commercial and, at large, extramarital sex, in order to justify why the scholarly and policy discourse made within this book should be deemed valuable.

ISLAMIC LAW, EXTRAMARITAL SEX AND THE INDONESIAN SOCIETY

Indonesia, like its neighbouring countries in Southeast Asia, has been internationally known for its rich culture, history, nature, wildlife and beautiful landscapes (Divinagracia et al. 2012). I have been to Bandung and Bali. Indonesian and foreign nationals should be familiar with Bali, one of the most stunning and tourist-popular attractions that houses ample nature, historical and cultural heritage, and nightlife. Foreign nationals might not necessarily know the place of Bandung but Indonesian nationals should be familiar with the place. I used to take a train from the city of Jakarta to Bandung for a three-day trip and Bandung was reachable from the city of Jakarta in about two to three hours. Bandung is a popular domestic tourism destination, where Indonesian nationals can gain access to beautiful landscapes, wildlife and ample historical and cultural heritage. The historical and cultural heritage, along with the rich natural resources, are appealing factors that help Indonesia draw the influx of international tourists.

However, similar to neighbouring Southeast Asian countries, Indonesia is, simultaneously, infamous for its prevailing sex tourism economy, sex industry and sex trafficking activities (Suhud and Sya'Bani 2014). On 6 December 2022, Indonesia's parliament passed the criminal code to criminalize extramarital sex. The anti-extramarital sex legalization was established to help reinforce Indonesia's, following Islamic Law, stance of disallowing sexual behaviours beyond marital relationships. Those who engage in extramarital sex, per the criminal code, are sentenced to up to a year in prison (Otte 2022).

In Indonesia, Islam has been known as the predominant religion, in which the nation has been recognized as the largest Muslim country in the world. Per the socio-religious contexts, extramarital sex is deemed an affair that violates the social, religious and moral values of Indonesia (Riswanda,

Mills, and Nantes 2017). The Indonesian government has enacted tight measures against the violation of adultery and its related activities (Fuadi et al. 2022). Here the Indonesian government wants to protect the integrity of marital relationships, prompting marital respect and dignity and reducing the occurrence of immoral behaviours in relation to extramarital sex. Here this book primarily refers to extramarital sex to commercial sex performed beyond a marital relationship. Beyond commercial sex, incidences of premarital sex, for example, are fairly common among Indonesian underage cohorts. I acknowledge that extramarital sex can occur in a variety of forms. However, given the focus of this book on Indonesian prostitution contexts, I predominantly draw my investigation on extramaritally commercial sex, especially in Chapters 3 and 4.

Criminalizing extramarital sex is one of Indonesia's most significant charges against the practice of adultery. Here according to the legal context, any Indonesian nationals engaging in sexual activity outside of their marital relationships can be sanctioned and imprisoned by law (Supardin and Syatar 2021). Such criminalization aims to prevent Indonesian nationals' practice of immoral behaviours, as well as contain the spread of sexually transmitted diseases by barring the Muslim-majority country from following the footsteps of Thailand and Cambodia to experiencing HIV/AIDS epidemics (Magnani, Riono, and Nurhayati 2010).

Along with imprisonment, Indonesian nationals violating extramarital sex also face fines and public shaming and may encounter punitive terms of being whipped with a rattan cane in some provinces (O'Donnell, Utomo, and McDonald 2020). In addition to these criminal sanctions, Indonesian nationals being caught violating extramarital sex could face societal dishonour and ostracism (ibid.). Seconding the arguments, owing to my Catholic affiliation, my ex-girlfriend and her family, who were living in Bekasi, a province next to the city of Jakarta, were subject to subtle or verbal forms of public shaming. This is because relationships between Indonesian Muslims with foreign non-Muslims are deemed a cultural and religious taboo in less-developed Indonesian areas. In regions beyond the city of Jakarta and Java where Chinese Indonesian and foreign non-Muslims can rarely be seen, public shaming serves as a form of significant informal social control that influences how Indonesian Muslim populations behave. The next chapter will discuss informal social control, outlining how such a social instrument is used to keep people away from expressing delinquency.

Indonesia's extramarital sex criminalization has drawn polarized opinions. Supporters believe that criminalization is a cornerstone to help protect the integrity and trust of marital relationships by attenuating the rates of immoral, betrayal behaviours. Dissidents, however, deem criminalization as an act that infringes upon personal freedoms (Bastari and Bastari 2017). Regardless of the public noise, Indonesia's extramarital sex criminalization is an example that demonstrates the prioritization of the Indonesian government of highlighting and upholding its religious, social and cultural values that aim to protect healthy marriage institutions and, more importantly, champion the practice of moral behaviours in accordance with Islamic law. While personal freedoms are deemed a pivotal international human right, the Indonesian government believes Indonesian nationals have to avoid any act of sexual misconduct as these behaviours, outlined by Islamic law, are significantly immoral and socially undesirable in Indonesian contexts (Fauk et al. 2021).

Indonesia is a culturally, ethically and religiously diverse country housing over 260 million people; the majority of them practise Islam. Indonesia's parliament has long been implementing laws and regulations to strengthen Indonesian citizens' expression of attitudes or practices of behaviours that are compatible with Islamic values and principles. Indonesia's criminalization of extramarital sex is one of the examples that demonstrates the efforts of Indonesia's parliament to strictly promote Islamic values. Islamic law is alternatively known as Sharia—a set of religious laws that Muslims follow. Sharia is formed and developed based on the Quran and the Hadith, referring to the teachings and actions of the Prophet Muhammad. By promoting Sharia law, Muslims are guided to live in a manner that follows the teachings of Islam (Munabari 2018). The development and legislation of extramarital sex criminalization are formed as per Islamic principles, where such a form of sexual misconduct is highly condemned as a moral sin. The Quran clearly states that any form of sexual activity outside of marital relationships is forbidden (Davies 2014). Here all extramarital sexual relationships are viewed as a violation of Islamic law. Indonesia's parliament passing the criminal code against any practice of extramarital sex is regarded as a support for Islamic law. The law delivers a strong message on behalf of Indonesia's parliament that Indonesian nationals' engagement in extramarital sex has to be sanctioned in order to uphold Islamic values and principles in Indonesian society.

The anti-extramarital sex law can be, furthermore, deemed legislation to protect the rights of women and girls in Indonesian society. Extramarital sexual activities can often result in negative consequences against female cohorts. These consequences include unintended and unwanted pregnancies, sexually transmitted diseases infections and social stigmatization against females who commit extramarital sex (Panjaitan 2019). Criminalizing extramarital sex helps deter Indonesian nationals' practice of sexual activities beyond marital relationships in the hope of helping maintain or improve women's rights and dignity nationwide.

Indonesia's anti-extramarital sex law is, in sum, a reflection of the commitment of Indonesia's parliament to promoting Islamic law and enforcing Islamic principles in society. While the law has drawn international controversies, primarily based on the violation of personal freedoms, Indonesia's parliament believes criminalization itself serves as an essential part of Indonesia's legal system. By criminalization, the Indonesian government encourages Indonesian nationals to live in accordance with Islamic teachings.

PROSTITUTION AND SEX TRAFFICKING IN INDONESIA

Prostitution and sex trafficking in any form are a violation of human rights and damage the dignity of humankind. Yet, prostitution and sex trafficking have been prevailing issues in Indonesia (Sutinah and Kinuthia 2019). The United Nations defines human trafficking as:

> the recruitment, transportation, transfer, harbouring or receipt of persons by means of threat or use of force or other forms of coercion, of abduction, of fraud, of deception, of the abuse of power or of a position of vulnerability or of the giving or receiving of payments or benefits to achieve the consent of a person having control over another person, for the purpose of exploitation (European Commission n.d.).

Indonesian women and children, especially those who are of underprivileged, impoverished and rural origins, are forced into prostitution where their bodies are sexually exploited by commercial sex clients as a form of profit-earning business (Iqbal and Gusman 2015). As Indonesia's parliament recently passed the criminal code of criminalizing extramarital sex within the country, this book visits the problems of prostitution and sex trafficking in Indonesian contexts and explores how such societal issues are affected by criminalization per se.

While prostitution is illegal in Indonesia, the country, like neighbouring nations in Southeast Asia, houses ample red-light districts—areas that openly practise commercial sex. Many sex tourists visit Indonesia, especially the cities of Jakarta and Bali, for commercial sex (Putra and Januraga 2020).

Given the significant demand for sexual transactions, ample women and children of underprivileged backgrounds are, coercively or voluntarily, driven to enter the sex industry as prostitutes. Normally, these sex workers suffer from poverty, unemployment, undereducation, domestic abuse and gender-based discrimination and stigmatization (Amalia 2018). With the rampant, longstanding commercial sex activities in red-light districts, the Indonesian government, despite criminalizing extramarital sex, experiences practical difficulties in enforcing the law.

Along with socio-economic factors, the weak law enforcement and justice systems, corrupt government officials and poor governance are additional reasons why Indonesia faces difficulties in cracking down on its sex industry (Buttle, Davies, and Meliala 2016). Without tight law enforcement and anti-prostitution crackdown at both the national and local levels, women and children of underprivileged backgrounds continue to see sex work as their last resort for income whenever their job opportunities in the conventional labour market have been highly limited. Women and children may also be lured to be sex trafficked, where the traffickers make fake promises of offering disadvantaged cohorts better life chances (Sutinah and Kinuthia 2019). Those who are tricked by sex traffickers often end up working as forced sex labour, in which they are sexually, physically and financially exploited. Given the weak law enforcement and justice systems, the Indonesian government has insufficiently penalized whoever is involved in prostitution and sex trafficking, such as commercial sex clients, pimps, sex traffickers, and conventional sex and entertainment establishment owners (Sohn 2019). With these parties assuming little to no legal responsibilities concerning their engagement in sexual transactions, Indonesia can hardly feasibly alleviate or eradicate the commercial sex industry. Women and children facing chronic or transitory social and economic disadvantages are continuing at high risk of experiencing sexual exploitation.

Sexual crime groups and sex traffickers usually target women and children in remote rural areas who appear to be significantly financially disadvantaged. They promise to offer these women and children desirable employment or education opportunities in cities. Given their constant financial hardships and underaged cohorts' immaturity, ample women and girls fall prey to sex traffickers (Wismayanti et al. 2019). These victims are forced to work as prostitutes or be involved in the production of, child or not, pornographic content. The profits are kept by sex traffickers or pimps, leaving the sexually exploited victims with no financial returns. Child and/or adult sex trafficking is a devastating experience for sexually exploited victims. Victims are at high risk of developing physical and emotional trauma, unintended and unwanted pregnancies, violent and life-threatening encounters and sexually transmitted diseases (Lyneham and Larsen 2013).

To date, according to the Global Slavery Index, Indonesia ranks 66th in the world concerning the prevalence of modern slavery, including sex slavery. Here Indonesia has an estimated 70,000 to 80,000 victims of, child and adult, sex trafficking (U.S. Embassy & Consulates in Indonesia 2021). The United Nations Children's Fund (UNICEF) has been working closely with Southeast Asian governments and non-governmental organizations (NGOs), including the Indonesian government, to collaboratively prevent and mitigate the problems of child sex trafficking by enhancing public awareness, capacity building and partnership formation against organized sex crimes to take place in Indonesia (Davy 2014). However, despite the existing endeavours, so long as the socio-economic and institutional root causes, briefly mentioned above, of prostitution and sex trafficking are not addressed properly, fully and timely, more women and children will be sexually exploited in the long term. Prostitution and sex trafficking, especially those where children are involved, must not be overlooked, as such sex crime has catastrophic impacts on children's lifelong development and Indonesia's moral fibre.

COMMERCIAL SEX, EXTRAMARITAL SEX CRIMINALIZATION AND ISLAMIC LAW

Extramarital sex criminalization applies to Indonesian nationals of all ages, including minors. Here child prostitution and child sex trafficking are sexual exploitations that involve the engagement of minors. The prevalence of child prostitution, child sex trafficking and child sex tourism are salient sexual offences that violate extramarital sex criminalization (Lindquist 2010). Minors are sexually exploited for financial gains, breaching the social, moral and religious values that such criminalization per se seeks to uphold. As discussed, involvement in child sex trafficking often encompasses the acts of using force, fraud and/or coercion, exacerbating the perpetrators' levels of criminality.

In response, the Indonesian government has applied interventions correspondingly. For example, the 2007 anti-trafficking law was enacted, the anti-trafficking police units have been established and social intervention programmes have been arranged and delivered over time to raise awareness of child sex trafficking (Kosandi et al. 2019). Despite the endeavours of the

Indonesian government, child prostitution and sex trafficking have been persisting in Indonesia. Here minors often encounter poverty, poor living conditions, a lack of employment opportunities and a shortage of education chances. Without addressing these socio-economic root causes of child prostitution in a sustainable, comprehensive manner, perpetrators (given the loose legal and justice mechanisms) are often not held accountable for their sexual offences.

Child prostitution and sex trafficking in Indonesia constitute severe violations of Indonesia's anti-extramarital sex legislation. Here significant controversies have been sparked owing to the fact that commercial sex is breaching moral, social and religious principles outlined by international human rights organizations and Islamic law, in addition to the significant physical, psychological, sexual and emotional harms such sexual offences impose on underage cohorts (Sutinah and Kinuthia 2019).

Islamic law plays a major role in defining Indonesia's social and political fabric. Child prostitution and child sex trafficking are social ills that are both abhorrent and illicit per Islamic and Indonesian laws. Such sexual offences significantly violate the injunctions against adultery, rape and exploitation as stated in the Qur'an (Yunus et al. 2021). Given the religious and legal violations, child prostitution and child sex trafficking are in part addressed and discussed in this book, allowing my engagement in the scholarly discourse on how prostitution and sex trafficking are socio-economically and institutionally constructed, in addition to my suggestion of how a process of deconstruction can be applied.

In Indonesia, ample poor, rural children who are sex trafficked are forced into the sex trade by their parents, relatives or guardians. Here these senior figures are enticed by the promise of financial compensation so long as they sell the children into the sex trade (Suryaningsi et al. 2021). When Indonesia's legal system has long been denounced for being ineffective and inconsistent in prosecuting sex crime groups, many offenders deem Indonesia and Southeast Asia at large as safe havens that allow them to commit sexual offences without bearing any legal consequences (Nuraeny 2017). Tackling prostitution and curbing sex trafficking, in addition, require collaborative efforts from a range of actors in society, including the central government, local governing agencies, NGOs and law enforcement units (Zimmerman and Kiss 2017). When inter-agency or inter-departmental coordination and cooperation, which will be discussed in detail in Chapter 4, have been insufficient, prostitution and related sexual exploitation continue to prevail in the Indonesian market.

This book will elaborate on how Indonesia has to endeavour to provide better access to life chances to disadvantaged populations, especially women and children. These life chances include education, employment and healthcare opportunities for impoverished families living in poverty in both cities and villages. Also, this book will explore how Indonesia's practice of Islamic law should be strengthened in order to ensure that child prostitution, child sex trafficking and other forms of child sexual exploitation are mitigated and eventually contained sustainably. I will also highlight how, for example, law enforcement agencies have to be empowered and equipped with more sufficiently accessible and usable resources to arrest, investigate, interrogate and prosecute sexual offenders. Moreover, I will engage in a policy-oriented discussion on how Indonesia should promote public awareness campaigns that educate the general public about the dangers, risks and costs of the involvement or initiation of prostitution and sex trafficking. The general public is entitled to the right to be well-informed about the legal, moral and religious consequences of engaging in commercial sex activities, including how involvement in sex work severely breaches the recently enacted anti-extramarital sex law in Indonesia.

By writing this book, I hope to inform how Indonesia can tighten its socio-economic and institutional mechanisms that help better protect the human rights entitled to all domestic citizens. I will suggest policy recommendations in the hope of helping Indonesia build a society which is just, equitable, habitable and sustainable, given my primary research interest in engaging in policy examination of and discourse on how sustainability can be built or consolidated. By systematically and strategically addressing the issues related to organized sex crimes, Indonesia can construct and strengthen its sustainable future where human and child rights are more respected.

SOCIAL, RELIGIOUS AND HISTORICAL CONTROVERSIES OF PROSTITUTION

Prostitution, especially child prostitution, has been drawing significant, multi-faceted controversies in Indonesian contexts. I highlight such controversies in social, religious and historical contexts. Socially speaking, child prostitution has resulted in a profound impact on Indonesian younger generations. Women and children involved in the sex industry usually come from low-income, rural and impoverished families. They, in most circumstances, find themselves constantly trapped in the vicious cycle of poverty and exploitation (Suyanto 2019). Given their underprivileged status and limited life chances, they easily fall prey to pimps, sex traffickers and brothel owners who lure them in with fake promises of better-conditioned economic or marital opportunities. In addition to tricking women and children into entering the sex industry with fake promises, victims may be forced into prostitution to help their households pay off unaffordable debts (Sutinah and Kinuthia 2019). Such exploitation always results in women and children suffering from physical, psychological, emotional and sexual health risks. These victims are traumatized with little to no support from their host society.

Religiously speaking, prostitution is a form of sexual misconduct that goes against Islamic teachings—where extramarital sex is prohibited and chastity and modesty are promoted. Many Indonesian nationals, who are predominantly Muslims, have failed to translate these Islamic teachings into actions, prompting the prevalence of sex work within the country. Despite the criminalization, prostitution operates in a grey area in Indonesia legally. Religious barriers (i.e., following Islamic teachings) alone fail to eradicate Indonesians' practice of commercial sex (Huda 2021). Here Indonesian public commonly views prostitution as a cultural taboo, but, simultaneously and ironically, turns a blind eye to sex work.

Historically speaking, child prostitution in Indonesian contexts could be traced back to Dutch colonialism. During that epoch, local women and children were constantly sexually abused and exploited by Dutch soldiers. Such a historical context of exploitation continued throughout Indonesia's era of military dictatorship, in which ample women and children were trafficked for commercial sex. Despite Indonesia's independence (in 1945), the problem of child prostitution has persisted (McGregor 2016). Here weak law enforcement and justice systems of the Indonesian government have deepened the vulnerability of women and girls who are at risk of being sexually exploited.

The Indonesian government has to take a more proactive approach to sanction sex traffickers, pimps and conventional sex establishment owners and support the rehabilitation of rescued sexually exploited victims. Indonesia's religious leaders should regularly and publicly condemn the acts of child prostitution and sex trafficking, in order to promote the importance of safeguarding the rights of minors. Indonesian society has to deliver more support and life chances to vulnerable women and girls, ensuring that they understand fully the risks and harms of engaging in commercial sex. These risks and harms include the religious violation of Islamic laws and the chances of being infected with sexually transmitted diseases.

In Indonesia, the government, religious institutions and groups and society should collaboratively confront the problems of prostitution and sex trafficking (Riswanda, Nantes, and Mills 2016). These actors have to actively safeguard the future, safety and health of Indonesia's children or younger generations, in order to allow them to develop their skill sets and knowledge base and become productive assets to society and the labour market in the long term.

INDONESIA'S TOLERANCE OF PROSTITUTION

Prostitution is, in theory and by law, illegal in Indonesia. However, in practice, prostitution has been widely tolerated in some parts of the country, especially in tourist hotspots like the city of Jakarta and Bali (Januraga et al. 2020). Indonesia's tolerance of prostitution, in many circumstances, translates into sexual exploitation. Sex trafficking and how such an illegal act damages victims' childhoods are examples of severe outputs of sexual exploitation. Indonesia's institutional loopholes, such as the problems of police corruption and loose law enforcement systems, are further indicators of Indonesia's tolerance of sex work (Riswanda, Mills, and Nantes 2017). While there are existing anti-prostitution and anti-extramarital sex laws, many of them are not consistently enforced. Indonesian society houses a significant level of stigmatization and public shaming against the delivery of commercial sex, rendering the difficulties for exploited women and children to come forward and report their sexual encounters and abuse (Davies 2014). Even when NGOs and localized governing agencies are responsible for curbing prostitution and sex trafficking in Indonesia, such organizations are often underfunded and understaffed, limiting their capacity to tackle sexual exploitation effectively.

While Indonesian and Islamic law severely and publicly denounces engagement in commercial sex, the country has long built a certain degree of tolerance for prostitution. Despite the tolerance, sex workers are significantly stigmatized, criticized and discriminated against, barring those who are constantly under threats of sexual and physical abuse from seeking help and support. Such a structural problem compounds the long-term harm sex work has imposed on prostitutes. Even if Indonesia has tolerated prostitution, the Indonesian government has to tighten its crackdown policies on sex work in order to rescue those being sexually trafficked from experiencing prolonged, detrimental harm. In this book, I acknowledge Indonesia, like neighbouring Southeast Asian countries, criminalizes but tolerates prostitution. I, in the next chapters, will explore the possible means of how the Indonesian government can strategically and systematically crack down on sex trafficking crimes, ensuring more disadvantaged women and girls not to be trapped in the vicious cycle of poverty, social underprivilege and sexual exploitation.

BOOK'S AIMS

This book responds to Indonesia's latest legislation that passed the criminal code criminalizing any act of extramarital sex on 6 December 2022 (Mao 2022). The formation of the arguments made in this book is based on the premise that, by criminalizing extramarital sex, the Indonesian government aims to, in part, crack down on the local prostitution industry to minimize any act of, child or not, sexual exploitation, prostitution and sex trafficking. The next few chapters will present how cracking down on the local or regional (i.e., Southeast Asia) prostitution industry cannot be accomplished by simply taking legislative actions. In the following chapter, I construct the theoretical framework of this book. Supported by the theoretical framework, throughout the book, I explain how commercial sex or alternative forms of sexual exploitation, such as live-streaming child pornography, are socio-economically and institutionally constructed. In addition to theoretical support, the understanding of commercial sex and sexual exploitation being socio-economically and institutionally constructed in Indonesian society is contextually established. For example, existing literature highlights that poverty, low education, ignorance and failure in governance are examples of factors that propel women and girls to be lured to enter the sex industry in Indonesia (Sutinah 2019). I thoroughly discuss how socio-economic empowerment and the reorganization of institutional mechanisms are pivotal policy goals that help Indonesia curtail the prevalence of the local sex industry in the long term. I detail how socio-economic and institutional endeavours, alongside legislative efforts, must be implemented simultaneously to crack down on the commercial sex industry in a sustainable fashion. Here I, in great detail, engage in the policy-oriented discussion to illustrate what policymakers should emphasize and prioritize to strategically eradicate the problems of sex work in phases within Indonesia. Ultimately, in the final chapter, I visit extramarital sex criminalization and draw associations between anti-extramarital sex and anti-commercial sex campaigns. I will argue how the betterment of cracking down on the sex industry is conducive to diminishing Indonesian nationals' likelihood of engaging in extramarital affairs. Moreover, when the prevalence of commercial sex activities is curtailed, an increased proportion of the

Indonesian population will be empowered and better socially protected and included, facilitating the country to build a more equitable, liveable and sustainable future.

FOCUSES OF THE FOLLOWING CHAPTERS

Chapter 2 will develop the theoretical framework of this book. I will introduce the social control theory, the cultural deviance theory, the social disorganization theory, the social learning theory, and poverty and crime, in order to explain what and how socio-economic and institutional influences propel the performance of commercial sex activities. I, moreover, will describe how each of these theories will be outlined and presented to justify the arguments made in the following chapters.

Chapter 3 will emphasize the discourse on the socio-economic construction of prostitution. I will rationalize how the encounter of poverty, a lack of informal and formal social control, a lack of positive socialization, peer influence, and the existence of cultural deviance all render disadvantaged Indonesian women and girls exposed to a disproportionately high risk of engagement in commercial sex. I, upon unveiling how commercial sex activities are socio-economically constructed and identifying existing relevant socio-economic policy gaps, suggest how disadvantaged populations at higher risks of engaging in commercial sex can be empowered to gain a fairer share of opportunities to follow the conventional, legal and morally acceptable route to enter the labour market.

Chapter 4 will highlight the discourse on the institutional construction of prostitution. I will rationalize how institutional barriers to compliance with morality have to be addressed. These institutional barriers include bad governance, a weak law enforcement system, and the practice of corruption. I will argue how the existence and prevalence of these institutional barriers worsen the socio-economic difficulties faced by those living in poverty and encourage the commitment to crimes, including entry into the sex industry. Upon unveiling how commercial sex activities are institutionally constructed and identifying existing, relevant institutional policy gaps, I will suggest how disadvantaged populations at higher risks of engaging in commercial sex can be institutionally barred from the expression of immorality and delinquency. As a result, those who intend to work, or are already working, in the sex industry are hampered from engagement in sexual transactions.

Chapter 5 will visit the latest legislation on passing the criminal code of criminalizing people who practise extramarital sex in Indonesia. I will argue how criminalization alone, without relevant socio-economic empowerment and well-organized institutional mechanisms presented in Chapters 3 and 4 respectively, cannot crack down on the sex industry. I believe that commercial sex activities should remain rampant in the domestic underground economy, or more local prostitutes will be trafficked to neighbouring sex tourism hubs, including Bangkok, Pattaya, Phnom Penh and Manila, to work as migrant sex workers. I will stress the importance of both local and regional collaboration to tighten intranational and international anti-prostitution policies to curtail the supply of sex workers within Indonesia and Southeast Asia at large.

There are a few books addressing prostitution, including child prostitution, sex trafficking and sex tourism in Southeast Asian contexts. Truong's (1990) *Sex, Money, and Morality: Prostitution and Tourism in Southeast Asia* and Lim's (1989) *The Sex Sector: The Economic and Social Bases of Prostitution in Southeast Asia* are monographs that analyse sex tourism and exploitation in detail. However, both monographs were published over three decades ago, so such arguments made may plausibly be dated and less relevant. Also, given the out-of-date status, both monographs fail to respond to Indonesia's latest extramarital sex criminalization enacted on 6 December 2022. Moreover, both monographs fail to focus on a primary or exclusive investigation of sexual exploitation commercially in Indonesian contexts. Tanielian's (2014) *Illicit Supply and Demand: Child Sex Exploitation in Southeast Asia* is a more updated monograph that assesses sexual exploitation in commercial settings. However, Tanielian fails to draw a primary or exclusive focus on Indonesian contexts. The lack of existing literature primarily or exclusively focusing on addressing sex tourism, prostitution and sex trafficking in Indonesia is understandable. This is because other neighbouring countries, led by Thailand, the Philippines, Cambodia and Vietnam, have been housing far larger sex trade markets and have been recognized as globally notorious sex tourism hubs. Therefore, I believe there is a need to develop this book to present the scholarly originality and significance of addressing the controversies in relation to the (de-)construction of sex work in Indonesia. This book should be deemed a valuable intellectual asset for Indonesian and Southeast Asian policymakers, Southeast Asian scholars and experts, and post- or undergraduate students specializing in Southeast Asian studies.

The next chapter will, in part, discuss people who are more socially engaged, including being religiously affiliated, and who enjoy a higher degree of social control that bars them from expressing delinquency. In Islam, extramarital affairs and engagement in commercial sex are significantly condemned. That being said, however, this book analyses why and how Indonesia's commercial sex activities remain rampant. This implies that the existence of social and religious control alone does not help completely shut down people's chances of expressing delinquency. I am keen on exploring what are the major drivers of prompting certain Indonesian populations to enter the sex industry. Also, I would like to assess how adding up these major drivers interdependently and collectively constructs the sex trade and work market in Indonesia.

References

Amalia, M. 2018. "Analysis of Factors Causing the Increase of Prostitution (Practice) in Cianjur Regency". *MIMBAR* 34, no. 2: 489–96.

Bastari, G., and G. Bastari. 2017. "The Indonesian Case". *Proceedings of the Third International Conference on Social and Political Sciences* (ICSPS 2017). https://doi.org/10.2991/icsps-17.2018.67

Buttle, J., G. Davies, and A. Meliala. 2016. "A Cultural Constraints Theory of Police Corruption: Understanding the Persistence of Police Corruption in Contemporary Indonesia". *Australian & New Zealand Journal of Criminology* 49, no. 3: 437–54.

Davies, S. 2014. "Surveilling Sexuality in Indonesia". In *Sex and Sexualities in Contemporary Indonesia*, edited by L. Bennett and S. Davies, pp. 29–50. London: Routledge.

Davy, D. 2014. "Understanding the Complexities of Responding to Child Sex Trafficking in Thailand and Cambodia". *International Journal of Sociology and Social Policy* 34, no. 11/12: 793–816.

Divinagracia, L., M. Divinagracia, and D. Divinagracia. 2012. "Digital Media-Induced Tourism: The Case of Nature-Based Tourism (NBT) at East Java, Indonesia". *Procedia - Social and Behavioural Sciences* 57, no. 1: 85–94.

European Commission. N.d. "Trafficking in Human Beings". https://home-affairs.ec.europa.eu/networks/european-migration-network-emn/emn-asylum-and-migration-glossary/glossary/trafficking-human-beings_en (accessed 19 March 2023).

Fauk, N., P. Ward, K. Hawke, and L. Mwanri. 2021. "HIV Stigma and Discrimination: Perspectives and Personal Experiences of Healthcare Providers in Yogyakarta and Beli, Indonesia". *Frontiers in Medicine* 6: 625787. https://doi.org/10.3389/fmed.2021.625787

Fuadi, M., M. Mahbub, I. Dewi, M. Safitry, and S. Sucipto. 2022. "The Historical Study of Prostitution Practices and Its Fiqh Analysis". *Jurnal of Daulat Hukum* 5, no. 2: 92–106.

Huda, M. 2021. "Sexual Harassment in Indonesia: Problems and Challenges in Legal Protection". *Law Research Review Quarterly* 7, no. 3: 303–14.

Iqbal, M., and Y. Gusman. 2015. "Pull and Push Factors of Indonesian Women Migrant

Workers from Indramayu (West Java) to Work Abroad". *Mediterranean Journal of Social Sciences* 6, no. 5: 167–74.

Januraga, P., J. Somers, H. Gesesew, and P. Ward. 2020. "The Logic of Condom Use in Female Sex Workers in Bali, Indonesia". *International Journal of Environmental Research and Public Health* 17, no. 5: 1627. https://doi.org/10.3390/ijerph17051627

Kosandi, M., V. Susanti, N. Subono, and E. Kartini. 2019. "Glorification Trap in Combating Human Trafficking in Indonesia: An Application of Three-Dimensional Model of Anti-Trafficking Policy". *International Journal of Humanities and Social Sciences* 13, no. 5: 669–74.

Lindquist, J. 2010. "Putting Ecstasy to Work: Pleasure, Prostitution, and Inequality in the Indonesian Borderlands". *Identities* 17, no. 2-3: 280–303.

Lyneham, S., and J. Larsen. 2013. "Exploitation of Indonesian Trafficked Men, Women and Children and Implications for Support". *Trends & Issues* 450: 1–7.

Magnani, R., P. Riono, and N. Nurhayati. 2010. "Sexual Risk Behaviours, HIV and Other Sexually Transmitted Infections among Female Sex Workers in Indonesia". *Sexually Transmitted Infections* 86: 393–99.

Mao, F. 2022. "Indonesia Passes Criminal Code Banning Sex Outside Marriage". *BBC News*. https://www.bbc.com/news/world-asia-63869078 (accessed 16 March 2023).

McCarthy, J. 2022. "Indonesia Passes a New Criminal Code That Prevents Extramarital Sex". *National Public Radio*. https://www.npr.org/2022/12/08/1141644859/indonesia-passes-a-new-criminal-code-that-prevents-extramarital-sex

McGregor, K. 2016. "Transnational and Japanese Activism on Behalf of Indonesian and Dutch Victims of Enforced Military Prostitution During World War II". *Asia-Pacific Journal* 14, no. 16: 1–21.

Munabari, F. 2018. "The Quest of Sharia in Indonesia: The Mobilisation Strategy of the Forum of Islamic Society". *Contemporary Islam* 12: 229–49. https://doi.org/10.1007/s11562-018-0416-z

Nuraeny, H. 2017. "Trafficking of Migrant Workers in Indonesia: A Legal Enforcement and Economic Perspective of Prevention and Protection Efforts". *European Research Studies Journal* 20, no. 4B: 16–26.

O'Donnell, J., I. Utomo, and P. McDonald. 2020. "Premarital Sex and Pregnancy in Greater Jakarta". *Journal of Population Sciences* 76, no. 13. https://doi.org/10.1186/s41118-020-00081-8

Otte, J. 2022. "'It's Absurd': Indonesians React to New Law Outlawing Sex Outside Marriage". *The Guardian*. https://www.theguardian.com/world/2022/dec/09/indonesians-react-to-new-law-outlawing-sex-outside-marriage

Panjaitan, A. 2019. "Model of Prevention of Adolescent Unwanted Pregnancy in Indonesia: Review Article". *International Journal of Research in Law, Economic and Social Sciences* 1, no. 2: 60–73.

Parker, L. 2016. "The Theory and Context of the Stigmatisation of Widows and Divorcees (*Janda*) in Indonesia". *Indonesia and the Malay World* 44, no. 128: 7–26.

Putra, G., and P. Januraga. 2020. "Social Capital and HIV Testing Uptake among Indirect

Female Sex Workers in Bali, Indonesia". *Tropical Medicine and Infectious Disease* 5, no. 2: 73. https://doi.org/10.3390/tropicalmed5020073

Riswanda, R., Y. Nantes, and J. Mills. 2016. "Re-Framing Prostitution in Indonesia: A Critical Systemic Approach". *Systemic Practice and Action Research* 29: 517–39. https://doi.org/10.1007/s11213-016-9379-2

———, J. Mills, and Y. Nantes. 2017. "Prostitution and Human Rights in Indonesia: A Critical Systemic Review of Policy Discourses and Scenarios". *Systemic Practice and Action Research* 30: 213–37. https://doi.org/10.1007/s11213-016-9393-4

Rojanapithayakorn, W. 2006. "The 100% Condom Use Programme in Asia". *Reproductive Health Matters* 14, no. 28: 41–52.

Sohn, K. 2019. "More Educated Sex Workers Earn More in Indonesia". *Feminist Economics* 25, no. 3: 201–23.

Suhud, U., and N. Sya'Bani. 2014. "Halal Sex Tourism in Indonesia: Understanding the Motivation of Young Female Host to Marry with Middle Eastern Male Tourists". *Journal of Economics and Sustainable Development* 5, no. 25: 91–95.

Supardin, S., and A. Syatar. 2021. "Adultery Criminalisation Spirit in Islamic Criminal Law: Alternatives in Indonesia's Positive Legal System Reform". *Samarah: Jurnal Hukum Keluarga dan Hukum Islam* 5, no. 1: 913–27.

Suryaningsi, S., W. Warman, L. Komariyah, N. Nurlaili, W. Mulawarman, Y. Hudiyono, and A. Thaba. 2021. "Legal Protection and Rehabilitation of Victims of Child Trafficking with the Purpose of Prostitution in Indonesia". *Journal of Legal, Ethical and Regulatory Issues* 24, no. 6: 1–16.

Sutinah, S. 2019. "Trafficking of Women and Children in East Java, Indonesia". *Journal of International Women's Studies* 20, no. 9: 94–106.

———, and K. Kinuthia. 2019. "Trafficking Women and Children in East Java, Indonesia". *Journal of International Women's Studies* 20, no. 9: Article 9. https://vc.bridgew.edu/jiws/vol20/iss9/9

Suyanto, B. 2019. "'Grey Chicken': Female Students as Exploitation Victims in the Commercial Sex Industry". *Journal of International Women's Studies* 20, no. 2: Article 13. https://vc.bridgew.edu/jiws/vol20/iss2/13

U.S. Embassy and Consulates in Indonesia. 2021. *Trafficking in Persons Report – Indonesia: Tier 2*. https://id.usembassy.gov/our-relationship/official-reports/2021-trafficking-in-persons-report/#:~:text=Traffickers%20increasingly%20use%20online%20and,the%20Riau%20Islands%20bordering%20Singapore (accessed 16 March 2023).

Wismayanti, Y., P. O'Leary, C. Tibury, and Y. Tjoe. 2019. "Child Sexual Abuse in Indonesia: A Systematic Review of Literature, Law and Policy". *Child Abuse & Neglect* 95: 104034. https://doi.org/10.1016/j.chiabu.2019.104034

Yunus, N., S. Nurhalimah, L. Nasution, and S. Romlah. 2021. "Human Trafficking in Indonesian Migrant Workers as an Extra-Ordinary Crime". *International Journal of Law* 7, no. 6: 44–49.

Zimmerman, C., and L. Kiss. 2017. "Human Trafficking and Exploitation: A Global Health Concern". *PLoS Medicine* 14, no. 11: e1002437. https://doi.org/10.1371/journal.pmed.1002437

2

Theoretical Framework

ABSTRACT

This chapter constructs the theoretical framework of this book. Here I introduce the social control theory, the cultural deviance theory, the social disorganization theory, the social learning theory, and poverty and crime, in order to explain what and how socio-economic and institutional influences propel the practice of commercial sex activities. I describe how each of these theories is outlined and presented in order to justify the arguments made in the following chapters concerning the socio-economic and institutional construction of sex work.

INTRODUCTION

This book engages in the sociological discourse on the (de-)construction of extramarital sex in commercial forms in Indonesia. I explain and address related social theories such as social control and social learning theories and the discussion about the nuanced relationships between poverty and crime in order to support my declaration of how prostitution and sex trafficking occur and persist in Indonesian contexts from a socio-economic perspective. Also, I apply additional theories named cultural deviance and social disorganization theories in order to support the rationalization of how prostitution and sex trafficking are both socio-economically and institutionally constructed. So long as how sex work is being constructed is detailed and clarified, I, in this book, am allowed to suggest how deconstruction should be practised.

SOCIAL CONTROL THEORY

The justification of how juvenile and adult cohorts express criminality or delinquency can be supported by the social control theory. According to the theory, those expressing criminality or delinquency often lack the social forces to harness them from presenting deviance in terms of their behaviours. The social control theory states that people are discouraged from taking part in criminality or delinquency by their social bonds to society (Agnew 1991). Negative life events, such as poor treatment by others (like parents, teachers and peers), lessen the strength of social control over people's criminality or delinquency. For example, when parents and teachers tend to apply devaluing and demeaning approaches to educate the younger generations, the latter cohorts are at higher risk of developing substantial strains that foster their expression of criminality and delinquency. Those who consistently encounter parental absence, denial or rejection, in addition to whoever encounters school and peer bullying, are major drivers of the diminished levels of social bonds to communities and society. As a result, these less socially controlled cohorts are at higher risk of performing criminality or delinquency (Bao et al. 2014). Those coming from impoverished, remote and rural households where parents may sell them to do hard labour or into the sex trade in childhood may plausibly lack the encounters with conventional others that can support their development of social control. As a result, such cohorts are prompted to practise or express criminality and delinquency.

Conventionally, the social control theory is assessed by three scales. These are (1) engagement in school activities, (2) parental supervision, and (3) parental attachment (Hawkins and Weis 2015; Hoffmann 2002). Beyond these three scales, other positive interpersonal relationships can also help strengthen people's development of social control. Cohorts encountering negative or an absence of parenting and a shortage of education opportunities are given limited opportunities to be schooled and learn what behaviours are deemed rightful and socially desirable. Not only are these less positively socialized less aware of the rightful and wrongful behaviours but they are deprived of opportunities to construct positive social or interpersonal relationships that are conducive to their consolidation of social control to harness them from expressing criminality and delinquency. Worse still, these cohorts experience an insufficiency of psychological and emotional support from parent-child communications, parenting, schooling or peer interactions. Due to the psychological and emotional deprivation, these socially distanced cohorts may see the expression of criminality or delinquency as an alternative channel for them to form social relationships with delinquents and become socially accepted.

In more privileged and well-resourced households, cohorts are less incentivized to express criminality and delinquency because they are entitled to stronger parental attachment and more positive parent-child relationships. A reduction in parental attachment does not necessarily minimize cohorts from, if appropriate, having opportunities to gain access to delinquents. However, those enjoying better parental attachment are discouraged from forming relationships and connections with the delinquents that they meet owing to their compliance with conventional, moral beliefs (Bao et al. 2014). A shortage of socialization acted by parents and teachers may trigger the expression of amoral beliefs and behaviours, while socialization initiated by delinquents may lead to the possible outcomes of being tempted to violate the laws (Agnew 1991). So long as the conventional social bond is weak or inadequate, cohorts care less about how important, trustable figures, such as parents and teachers, view them, rendering their higher chances of engaging in criminality or delinquency. Such vulnerable cohorts demonstrate a lower level of commitment to the investment in conventional lines of action, such as progressing academically and pursuing career advancement. Their insufficiency of incentivization to commit conventional behaviours and norms, according to the social control theory, compounds their likelihood of developing deviance (Pitt and Walker 2022). These cohorts are at high risk of acting criminally or delinquently owing to their assumption of lower costs when expressing themselves in a socially undesirable way. People who are systematically marginalized and discriminated against, therefore, lack life chances and promising, positive academic and professional trajectories and, hence, sacrifice less if they express criminality or delinquency (ibid.).

People engaging in more family or school activities and establishing more positive social bonds and relationships with parents, teachers, peers and neighbours present fewer outcomes that are socially perceived as negative or disdained (ibid.). In order to bar people from expressing criminality and delinquency, in addition to promoting their health, well-being and development, people should be encouraged to engage more in extracurricular activities or social events organized within communities or villages. However, here those from impoverished, rural and remote origins may lack the necessary financial and time resources to take part in extracurricular activities as they are vulnerable to performing child hard labour to support their households' subsistence needs. As an outcome, those who are underprivileged are at higher risk of expressing criminality and delinquency.

This book, thus far, explains briefly how criminality and delinquency, and their associations with social disadvantages, are socially constructed and reproduced. I will further elaborate on such contexts in Chapter 3. People experiencing chronic poverty or financial pressure are prompted to perform less socially acceptable behaviours. They usually enjoy a lesser degree of social control but a heightened level of financial strain, engendering their risks of expressing criminality and delinquency as a means to seek social values or secure financial gains. People who are vulnerable to the expression of criminality and delinquency are less likely to provide adequately positive parenting to the next generation, propelling the formation of intergenerational reproduction of social disadvantages, criminality and delinquency. Unless more apt interventions are applied to discourage people from continually expressing criminality and delinquency, the social construction and reproduction natures of deviance are likely to harm the development of a sustainable future for Indonesia.

In the following section of the social disorganization theory, I will elaborate on how the formation of disorganized communities attenuates the practice of social control and, thus, encourages the expression of criminality and delinquency (Bellair 2017; Hoffmann 2002). Whenever local communities are more underregulated and disorganized, more opportunities for criminality and delinquency are made available. Natives and residents living in these neighbourhoods are, as a result, exposed to higher risks of behaving criminally. Moreover, in these disorganized communities, the levels of the social bond to harness people from expressing criminality and delinquency are attenuated as the degree of supervision and the availability of positive interpersonal attachments are more tenuous (Hoffmann 2022). These circumstances facilitate the growth of crime and delinquency.

From a sociological perspective, conformity is attained through socialization and the construction of social bonds. These bonds formed between people and societies include attachment, involvement, belief and commitment. As long as conformity is appropriately presented, championed and adopted by people, their levels of social bonds will enhance and the risks of expressing criminality or delinquency will diminish (Wiatrowski, Griswold, and Roberts 1981). The importance of values of promoting conformity at multi-faceted (including family, community and societal) levels underpin the need to develop this book—in order to recommend local policymaking that the Indonesian government and local governing agencies should take into account to strengthen the levels of conformity Indonesian nationals hold.

While social disadvantage alone is not associated with the expression of delinquency, the shortage of social control experienced by socially underprivileged cohorts is driving them to practise deviance (Junger and Tremblay 1999). It is, therefore, important for Indonesian policymakers to take more initiatives to improve the living standards of those experiencing social disadvantages. When ameliorating their living standards, Indonesian policymakers have to ensure that positive social bonds are in place. If not, even if the socially disadvantaged cohorts are empowered, their shortage of social control renders their persistence in experiencing risks of criminal and delinquent expression. Educating parents and parents-to-be to develop apt parenting skills is, hence, deemed a pivotal means to reinforce the next generation's levels of social control. With an enhanced degree of social control, people are less likely to express criminality and delinquency as they have better discipline and higher levels of conformity.

Per the social control theory, people are encouraged to take part in more conventional activities, including socio-recreational events organized by religious groups, school attendance or off-work gathering opportunities initiated by work units. Taking part in these social events helps facilitate people's development of the social network. In addition to school and work units, the conventional social network can be built or extended within familial and community settings (Karstedt and Kai 2000; Rogers and Pridemore 2016; Wiatrowski, Griswold, and Roberts 1981). A major factor in expressing criminality and delinquency is owing to the lack of peer attachment among delinquents or criminals (Wiatrowski, Griswold, and Roberts 1981). Whenever people are given more inconsistent and/or inadequate opportunities to form and maintain positive peer relationships, they are inclined to behave in a socially undesirable or unacceptable manner. Stronger social bonds and more positive, healthier interpersonal relationships are, therefore, significant deterrents to disincentivizing people from expressing criminality and delinquency.

At the family level, for the purpose of building a more constructive interpersonal relationship with children, it is noteworthy that parents are required to apply appropriate rearing approaches. For example, highly responsive parenting tends to help express and deliver more parental warmth. Parents have to avoid presenting any form of coercion and intimidation when practising their parenting. They should be aware of the importance of delivering a certain level of autonomy to their children by allowing their children to develop a greater degree of independence, social competence and self-regulation. Such parenting approaches help strengthen positive, constructive parent-child social relationships and bonding, enabling the beneficiaries of appropriate parenting to build a higher level of social control (Hay 2006). International literature supports such a claim by showing that parental responsiveness attenuates juvenile delinquency in both Chinese and American contexts (Li, Liu, and Xia 2023). As a result, such contexts help suggest how the possession and development of social control can be intergenerationally reproduced, benefiting the younger generations living in healthy families to keep themselves away from expressing criminality or delinquency.

Furthermore, labour market participation affects people's formation and consolidation of attitudes towards conformity (Wadsworth 2000). Delinquent behaviours may disrupt occupational trajectories in the labour market, in part, due to the lack of self-discipline and conformity, leading to a risk of being unemployed. While keeping human capital and demographic traits constant, delinquents are far more likely than non-delinquents to be unemployed (Carter 2019). In the next chapter, I will discuss how people, especially women and children, who are continuously and systematically discriminated against in the labour market are prone to exercise a lesser degree of social, moral and religious conformity and, as a result, are inclined to express the involvement in criminality or delinquency. The form of criminality or delinquency I primarily focus on in this book is commercial sex engagement. There I will explain how those who are occupationally discriminated against are at higher risk to be tempted to earn quick and easy money from commercial sex activities. They are, therefore, more vulnerable to being commodified as sex labour. Such sex labourers enjoy lower degrees of social control and are less likely to commit themselves to conformity and conventional values, beliefs and perceptions. They, hence, display more salient deviances in order to satisfy their own or their households' subsistence needs.

Child labourers experiencing physical and sexual exploitation and abuse on a regular basis have a disposition to express criminality and delinquency, owing to the fact that they are entitled to weaker bonds to conformity. Moreover, they are given more opportunities to perform deviance as these cohorts are primarily working and living in conventional sex and entertainment establishments that are surrounded by organized crimes. Therefore, they are tempted to engage in criminal or delinquent behaviours to some degree (Spruit et al. 2016; Wadsworth 2000). People participating in child labour are, in addition, entitled to limited educational opportunities. Less-educated cohorts are less committed to following conventional beliefs, values and perceptions. They, in general, develop a less satisfactory degree of conformity. Their limited education opportunities restrict their desirability when entering the labour market. Better-conditioned job opportunities are, in most circumstances, not accessible to them, prompting their experience of longer-term occupational limitation, marginalization and even discrimination. Those who are continuously occupationally discriminated against and rejected are at higher risk of expressing criminality and delinquency, such as entering the sex industry. A positive labour market trajectory does not occur overnight. Indonesian policymakers have to intervene in the structural discrimination against underprivileged cohorts in both the educational and labour markets, in order to ensure that those who are on the verge of engaging in, underage or not, commercial sex are academically and occupationally empowered. More upskilling and reskilling opportunities have to be allocated to underprivileged cohorts shall local Indonesian policymakers hope to address the issues of sexual child labour in a timely and effective fashion. Human investment, especially human resources redistribution, has to be applied and delivered to facilitate the longer-term empowerment of underprivileged women and children. As a result, they would be more encouraged to conform to moral, religious and social values, minimizing their participation in the underground economy, such as the sex trade activities.

The association between the expression of criminality and delinquency and labour market participation are intergenerationally reproduced. Shall parents regularly experience negative life events at work, they might respect their parenting roles less and deliver less degree of parental care, supervision and warmth to their children (Wadsworth 2000). Supporting literature argues that a rise in parental stress can adversely alter parent-child interactions and worsen the quality of child upbringing. In the long term, families with a higher degree of parental stress usually heighten parenting-related difficulties, in part, caused by a growth of the application of inappropriate disciplinary strategies and physical abuse (Cusinato et al. 2020). As a result, negative parental socialization happens. Indonesian policymakers have to champion more positive labour market engagement (such as upskilling and reskilling labourers in order to allow them to be more occupationally included and be able to secure more respectful, conformed and better-conditioned jobs). When parents are more occupationally included, active and promising, their children are inclined to view them as role models and are more likely to be intergenerationally influenced to undertake legal, morally conformed and respected jobs upon their entry into the labour market. This means human investment in people's academic and occupational development brings more benefits than reducing their expression of criminality and delinquency. Here empowered cohorts are likely to influence the next generations to be active and engaged in the legal, conventional labour market. As a consequence, conformity can be intergenerationally reproduced.

Human investment in underprivileged cohorts facilitates their households' enjoyment of better occupational and financial stability and protection, owing to the simple fact that they are employed and salaried. Huang, Laing, and Wang (2004) argue that parents who are employed and salaried tend to offer more positive parenting and parental care, supervision and warmth to their children, relative to their counterparts who are unemployed. However, Hsin and Felfe (2014) argue paternal rather than maternal employment is conducive to the practice of positive parenting. Maternal employment reduces mothers' time spent with children, leading to a limited mother-child interaction opportunity and posing risks to children's development of adverse psychological and behavioural outcomes. Unemployment and the expression of criminality and delinquency are interrelated. The longer people remain unemployed, the more frustrated and strained they become and the more likely they will express criminality and delinquency (Huang, Laing, and Wang 2004). As a result, human investment is a prominent intervention that has to be universally applied in order to strengthen the financial stability and well-being of underprivileged households, minimizing their practice of juvenile delinquency.

The availability and accessibility of formal employment opportunities and the odds of expressing criminality or delinquency are negatively correlated. With the presence of more accessible formal, legal employment opportunities, more people would be occupationally included in the conventional labour market. As a result, they are less incentivized to undertake job opportunities in the underground, illegal economy (Huang, Laing, and Wang 2004). Supporting literature argues that employment lowers economic needs, disincentivizing people from committing poverty-stricken crimes such as robbery and theft (Duwe 2015). An additional study shows that adolescents in Chicago who were offered summer employment opportunities for 25 hours per week committed fewer violent crimes during the next 12 months, compared to their counterparts who were not undertaking any summer jobs (Heller 2014). Therefore, in addition to improving the levels of human investment, Indonesian policymakers have to address the structural, deep-seated problem of unequal power of relations (such as in the form of gender inequality). Here Indonesian policies have to ensure that not only are more underprivileged cohorts given the opportunities to be educated, but they are able to gain access to employment opportunities that they deserve on a non-discriminatory basis.

As a result, improving the accessibility of formal, conventional and legal job opportunities by changing the entrenched unequal power structure will be discussed in detail in the next chapter, in order to explain how people can be more occupationally engaged and included in a way that deters them from expressing criminality and delinquency.

In this book, Chapters 3, 4 and 5 will present recommended pro-poor interventions that aim at empowering the underprivileged cohorts' access to life chances. The application of such pro-poor interventions is necessary to change the long-term poverty, social disadvantages and systematic deprivation subjected by underprivileged cohorts. Also, in the following section about poverty and crime, I will delineate how the chronic issue of poverty is driving people who are financially insecure or marginalized to express criminality and delinquency. Applying prop-poor interventions is, therefore, deemed a means to help address people's expression of poverty-led criminality. Socio-economically deconstructing the practice of, child or adult, prostitution and sex trafficking is, therefore, a key scholarly output I am presenting in this book.

CULTURAL DEVIANCE AND SOCIAL LEARNING THEORIES

The cultural deviance theory is another theory that deserves some attention in this book. The understanding of the cultural deviance theory also helps facilitate the interpretation of the social learning theories. The cultural deviance theory is set based on the hypothesis that criminality and delinquency stem from learned beliefs that prompt the construction of thoughts in which expressing crime commitment is justifiable and socially appropriate in response to given social conditions (Costello 1997). Here I have to declare and highlight that such a hypothesis of the cultural deviance theory has widely been criticized and challenged by criminologists, claiming that the theory per se wrongly assumes human behaviours and cultural roles in deviance (Akers 1996). For example, the cultural deviance theory mistakenly assumes that every person fully internalizes social norms and complies with them; so long as such cultural norms shared by any social group are deviant by the standard of society, members of the social group will have the disposition to express criminality or delinquency (ibid.). Despite the criticisms and plausible inappropriate assumptions on human behaviours and tendencies, the introduction of the cultural deviance theory is a gateway to the examination of the social learning theory.

The social learning theory is designed to explain the initial act of deviance in certain ways. These include non-social reinforcement, the negative reinforcement of deviance through the avoidance of punishment and the imitation of others' deviance (Costello 1997). The social learning theory, unlike the cultural deviance theory, pays more attention to non-social sources of reinforcement in which a perfectly socialized actor fails to deviate from the cultural norms of their own social groups. Non-social reinforcement can be interpreted as the participation in behaviours that is incongruent with people's own normative standards (ibid.). Similar to theorists of the social control concepts, those advocating the social learning theory believe crime can be posited as being inherently reinforced and people who are given opportunities to take part in expressing criminality prefer doing so (ibid.). When there is a notion that delinquency is socially unacceptable, people tend to learn the negative consequences by expressing themselves in such a way. However, when there is a presence of a notion that delinquency is socially acceptable, those expressing themselves in such a way can, for example, enjoy prestige and status to a desirable degree. People being barred from accessing the opportunities to express their perceived "socially acceptable" delinquency will ignore the obstacles and present their deviance, because they believe their behaviours can result in preferable outcomes (ibid.).

Shall any blockages to success exist, deviant subculture will occur, causing the collective expression of criminality or delinquency to overcome such obstacles. People will find illegitimate chances to realize culturally approved goals or alternative means to reach such targets (ibid.). However, the cultural deviance theory over-relies on the examination of how behaviours are shaped through the influences of collective structural conditions on patterns of thinking and values. So long as such structural conditions no longer exist, the theory fails to explain why the patterns of thinking and values remain operating as independent drivers of crime. In Southeast Asia where people are educationally, financially and occupationally deprived and marginalized, they are propelled to express criminality and delinquency. Yet, whenever an adequate welfare package can be allocated to those of vulnerability, the cultural deviance theory fails to rationalize why a portion of delinquents continue to participate in, for example, commercial sex (ibid.). Here the cultural deviance theory contains some significant limitations, despite having valuable insights. I, therefore, compensate for the limitations by using alternative/additional theories, such as the social control theory and social learning theories, to support the construction of the theoretical framework. Here I declare how, in addition to social protection, social control and social influence are alternative social instruments that play roles in shaping people's conformity and/or expression of criminality and delinquency.

It is noteworthy that both cultural deviant and social learning theorists explain why there are higher crime rates located in regions where the cultural transmission of criminality and delinquency is salient and rampant. According to the social learning theory, people learn the definitions of delinquent and prosocial behaviours through contingencies of reinforcement operating in the socialization process. They are prompted to present behaviours that are socially and/or culturally appropriate and rewarding while avoiding the expression of traits or behaviours that are socially or culturally deemed inappropriate. Anticipating the reinforcement and sanction (de-)motivates people to express conformity or violation in certain ways (Akers 1996). According to the social learning theory, people are inclined to express criminality or delinquency should they hold any favourable definitions of their behaviours; or so long as they expect a desirable payoff or a low-risk punishment when acting in a deviant manner (ibid.). In this book, I will present the cultural deviance in Indonesia's tourist-popular locations where prostitution in any form is culturally tolerated to some degree. Countries within and beyond Southeast Asia have been regulating and tolerating commercial sex activities to a certain degree. Shaping a utopia where prostitution is completely prohibited, from a pragmatic standpoint and given the entrenched levels of poverty and/or socio-economic inequality, is unlikely to be feasible or even socially conducive in reality. Therefore, domestic women and girls who need to earn "quick and easy" money are less disincentivized from entering the sex industry as they may not necessarily deem engagement in commercial sex a highly socially, morally and religiously wrongful and sanctionable behaviour.

The contingencies of reward or sanction influence people's development and presentation of attitudes and behaviours over time. People are prompted to engage in or refrain from certain acts based on the social learning evaluation. They learn what sorts of actions can result in their entitlement to rewards. In many circumstances, these actions may be immoral and illegal (Akers 1996). For example, people are aware of the costs and harms of being trafficked to work as modern sex slaves. However, they may agree (or may be forced in some circumstances) to enter the sex trade as their decision helps their poor households pay off their debts. Moreover, people sometimes are well aware that their expression of criminality and delinquency is morally, legally and socially undesirable. However, whenever such an expression helps them with any form of social acceptance from strengthening their interpersonal relationships with peers or from acquiring instant psychological, emotional or financial relief, they are tempted to deliver deviance. Per the social learning theory, people's criminality and delinquency can be built through the process of imitation. So long as people join the membership of any social group, they have the disposition to behave like others to seek social acceptance (Matsueda 1997). Additionally, in circumstances where the expression of criminality and delinquency is rampant, the legal consequences of behaving in such ways may be relatively low because law enforcement authorities and local policymakers may build their tolerance levels of deviance. This book emphasizes how Indonesia has long been building some degree of tolerance of commercial sex, rendering the engagement in sex work, despite the illegal nature, to be bound by lower levels of legal consequences. The low legal costs of expressing criminality and delinquency compound people's willingness or tendency to engage in socially, legally and morally less acceptable behaviours.

In certain circumstances, the expression of criminality is rewarded (Matsueda 1997). In Southeast Asian contexts, for example, brothel owners reward child prostitutes of impoverished family backgrounds so long as they participate in commercial sex with clients. No matter whether child sex trafficking victims are aware of the legal consequences that, in theory, they are bearing when delivering sexual transactions, they, to some degree, accept their assigned roles to perform sex work with clients as such deviance helps their biological households to pay off their debts. In situations where undereducation, unemployment and poverty rates are undesirably high, crime tends to be rewarded. Such an argument is particularly applicable in settings where the social security system is poorly facilitated. With a shortage of social security, more unemployed, underemployed and less educated households are experiencing financial strains to satisfy their subsistence needs. Expressing criminality or delinquency is, as a result, seen as a rewarding means to help them secure financial relief either on a transitory or chronic basis (Hooghe et al. 2011). When participating in commercial sex, people who are rejected or denied in the conventional labour market are able to seek an alternative channel to secure financial gains. They are fully or partially aware of the costs or risks that they have to bear in the long run, despite the instant financial relief. These long-term costs and risks include the salient socio-cultural stigmatization against prostitutes, the possibility of infecting sexually transmitted diseases, the deepened detachment and distancing from the conventional labour market and the victimization from physical and verbal violence and abuse. These long-term costs and risks in association with sex work show why Indonesia, beyond religious consideration, has been maintaining a very limited tolerance of prostitution. Here the tolerance levels do not necessarily reflect the popularity of sex work. While Indonesia's tolerance levels of prostitution are kept at a low level, sex work, as mentioned, is rampant within and beyond Indonesia. It is pragmatically infeasible to practise zero-tolerance of prostitution in Southeast Asian contexts. However, Indonesia should actively tighten its regulation in addition to passing the anti-extramarital sex law in December 2022 in order to strictly regulate commercial sex.

SOCIAL DISORGANIZATION THEORY

To further enrich the sociological discussion of anti-extramarital sex and regulation of sex work, I introduce the social disorganization theory to support the discourse on how and why the expression of criminality and delinquency is popular in poorer, less regulated and more segregated communities. According to the social disorganization theory, poverty, residential instability, the shortage of social networks and ethnic heterogeneity, all hamper the neighbourhoods' capacity from refraining or controlling people's presentation of behaviours and traits in public. Consequently, people's risks of expressing criminality or delinquency may be facilitated (Kubrin and Weitzer 2003). Neighbourhood mechanisms like the construction of social ties and the encouragement of the exercise of social control are some major social assets that help attenuate crime rates within localities. Social ties and social control can help mediate the effects of exogenous sources of social disorganization on crime control. People collectively sanctioning or preventing the expression of criminality and delinquency through informal, shared surveillance in public is a kind of collective social control that helps reduce crime rates (Kubrin and Weitzer 2003). Wickes et al. (2013) argue that neighbourhoods with strengthened social ties enjoy a higher degree of collective efficacy and social cohesion, barring the emergence of delinquency and political/civic issues. Applying social control serves as a cornerstone to the intervention in restraining crime commitment, per the social disorganization theory (Warner 2003). The degree of the shared informal social control hints at the level of social cohesion, integration and trust within the corresponding communities, neighbourhoods or social groups. The more people are connected, integrated and trusted within the social settings; the lower crime rates should be recorded. This is because people tend to assume higher responsibilities to monitor the behaviours of one another in public spaces, ensuring that each of them is presenting themselves in a socially desirable or acceptable manner (Bellair 2017).

In addition to the possession of informal social control (for example, forming social ties), acquiring formal social control (for example, participation in organizational and community activities) facilitates collective surveillance to reduce crime commitment within communities, neighbourhoods and social groups (Sampson and Groves 1989). Promoting the formation of formal and informal ties, as a result, engenders the development of collective ability and willingness to tackle chronic societal problems, such as the victims of sex trafficking (ibid.). Here people who are socially tied to one another often form informal interpersonal agreements for the accomplishment of mutually desired goals. By constructing informal interpersonal agreements, people are inclined to supervise social activities within neighbourhoods, communities and social groups. For example, people tend to observe others' behaviours in public spaces and learn which locations or areas they should avoid walking past to lower their risks of facing any form of danger. With the possession of more informal social control, people are more likely to, in addition, question others who behave in ways that disrupt the social order of the neighbourhoods. They are prone to institutionally socializing children towards the practice of conventional, moral values as a circumstance that attenuates younger generations' risks of expressing criminality or delinquency (Bellair 2017). Social (dis)organization is, thus, significantly associated with the systematic networks of the formation or application of community-level social control (Sampson and Groves 1989).

In areas with higher levels of social organization, people may, moreover, work closely with police officers to identify community problems. Some forms of "street codes" may be developed within people, stating how they should behave in public to shape the collective values and acts in a socially desirable and valuable manner. Community policing serves as a pivotal social control means to limit one another's chance of breaking the laws or upsetting the existing social order. Consequently, local crime rates should fall (Kubrin and Weitzer 2003). It is noteworthy that existing literature argues community policing is effective only in communities with non-high crime rates. The outcomes of community policing are more satisfactory when such a strategy is applied in more organized, urbanized communities. In communities with high crime rates, exercising community policing is the least effective (Rukus, Warner, and Zhang 2018).

POVERTY AND CRIME

So far, I briefly address how, child or adult, sex trafficking and prostitution are poverty-driven. Further exploration of poverty-led sex crimes will be thoroughly addressed in the next chapter. In this section, I would like to theorize the associations between poverty and crime, in order to facilitate the presentation of the next chapter. Here I would like to take a macroeconomic perspective to indicate how the financial upheaval faced by underprivileged Indonesian women and children renders them at risk of engaging in commercial sex, despite the significant moral unacceptance and social disdain attached to prostitution.

Existing literature argues that poverty is associated with exposure to violence, growth of incarceration rates and the presentation of crime and aggression (Graif, Gladfelter, and Matthews 2014). In neighbourhoods and communities subjected to poverty, there are lower levels of social ties, cohesion and trust. Residents share less degree of awareness and responsibility to realize collective values, attitudes and goals of attenuating crime rates. Moreover, in these poor, underprivileged and under-resourced neighbourhoods, the law enforcement system often contains ample loopholes, enabling actors to take advantage of the broken legal, justice and institutional mechanisms to express criminality and delinquency (ibid.). Such circumstances reiterate the lack of social control within poor communities, leading to a heightened rate of crime.

In addition to the lack of legal consequences for the expression of criminality or delinquency, acting in a deviant manner may result in positive outcomes. In some contexts, the expression of criminality or delinquency can raise people's socio-economic well-being and occupational advancement (Pare and Felson 2014). For example, working as freelance sex workers in Indonesia allows university or high school girls to afford their tuition fees. In regions where there is a shortage of economic potential, available resources and regulations, organized crime groups may take advantage of the institutional and justice loopholes to expand their underground businesses in these areas, creating illegal economic opportunities for their own financial gains (Barona, Jimenez, and Melo 2019). For example, in areas with a slow pace of rural development, conventional labour markets and education opportunities are inadequate. Also, rural, remote areas are usually subject to poor governance and loose law enforcement systems. As a result, sex-organized crime groups can lure domestic, poor and socially disadvantaged women and children to provide commercial sex in order to help earn a lucrative source of financial gains.

Poverty is one of the major socio-economic root causes of crime, including sex work. In addition to poverty, economic inequality and the shortage of economic resources are some examples of indicators of higher crime rates (Barona, Jimenez, and Melo 2019; Fafchamps 2006). In economically less equal communities, the expression of criminality may be conducive to both privileged and less privileged groups. Privileged cohorts can easily capitalize on their leverage of the unequal power of relations to exploit the interests of their socially disadvantaged counterparts, such as luring the latter to work as hard labour, including sex labour. Less privileged cohorts, alternatively, find the expression of criminality a means to improve their financial well-being for both themselves and their rural households. A lack of conventional economic opportunities is, therefore, a factor in the occurrence of high crime rates. Underprivileged cohorts are systematically discriminated against and marginalized, where their opportunities to legitimately seek life chances from the education and conventional labour market are blocked. They have no better options than committing crimes in order to acquire resources and achieve goals that satisfy their households' needs (Pare and Felson 2014).

When people are living in less socially controlled, more socially disorganized and more economically disadvantaged communities or neighbourhoods, they often encounter the socialization process that renders their development of attitudes and traits in favour of crime commitment (ibid.). Socially disorganized and economically disadvantaged communities and neighbourhoods, therefore, often record high rates of criminal or delinquent expression (Hipp and Yates 2011). People living in these neighbourhoods tend to believe the use of violence, aggression, exploitation and delinquency is a legitimate means to reinforce their authority, and entitlement to social and economic rewards, and expand their social influences. These people experience fewer adverse consequences when deviance is practised, owing to the lack of regulation and broken localized justice system. They are, hence, going through a lesser extent of negative social learning processes to hamper their expression of criminality and delinquency. Social disorganization and poverty are interrelated to a large extent. People living in poverty, especially extreme poverty, are subject to a lack of food, subsistence crises and chronic starvation. They are financially desperate to find means to help support their families and their own subsistence needs. Such socio-economic setting consolidates their willingness to use violence, aggression, exploitation and criminal means to seek opportunities for survival (Papaioannou 2007; Pare and Felson 2014). The next two chapters will elaborate on how poverty, social disadvantages and social disorganization are part of the core root causes driving the incidences of poverty-led crime, including criminalized, underage or not, sex trafficking and prostitution.

CONCLUSION

The theoretical framework established in this chapter is beneficial to my justification, in the rest of this book, of how sex work is constructed in a multi-faceted fashion in Indonesian contexts. Supported by these introduced and discussed socio-criminological theories and relevant literature, this book explores the key responses of the Indonesian government should the government plan to alleviate or eradicate the engagement in commercial sex. Only by eliminating the root causes of sex work can the Indonesian government build a lower tolerance of extramarital sex in Indonesia in the long run. In the remaining chapters of this book, I address how lowering the tolerance of prostitution is far more complex than simply tightening the law enforcement operations against or raising the punitive terms of the criminalization of involvement in sex work. The Indonesian government has to incentivize those who are at risk of entering the sex industry to stay disciplined and behave socially desirable, and has to disincentivize those who are working in prostitution to leave sex work. Also, the Indonesian government has to address its structural governing challenges and reform its law enforcement and justice systems to foster the endeavours of cracking down on any commercial sex activities.

These are far easier said than done. However, to build a more sustainable future where no women and children, regardless of their origins, should be left behind, I developed this book that in part focuses on policy examination and recommendations to advocate and champion the crackdowns on the structural unequal power relations. Such unequal power relations result in, as presented throughout this book, the by-products of sex tourism, prostitution, intergenerationally reproduced socio-economic disadvantages, sexual health crises, physical abuse and exploitation, human rights violation, corruption, sexism and gender inequality. Therefore, so long as the Indonesian government can strategically, effectively and consistently crack down on its sex industry, these by-products can be addressed to some degree simultaneously. That is why, in this book, while I, as a sociologist, focus on using extramarital sex criminalization as a background to introduce and analyse the problems of sex work, I am assessing more, overt or covert, undesirable social issues that are related to prostitution and sex trafficking. These social issues are interrelated and interdependent to some degree.

When I am examining prostitution and sex trafficking, I hope readers can take a broader consideration of how the unequal power structure in Indonesian society and the adverse social by-products are developed, constructed and reproduced.

References

Agnew, R. 1991. "Longitudinal Test of Social Control Theory and Delinquency". *Journal of Research in Crime and Delinquency* 28, no. 2: 126–56.

Akers, R. 1996. "Is Differential Association/Social Learning Cultural Deviance Theory". *Criminology* 34, no. 2: 229–48.

Bao, W., A. Haas, X. Chen, and Y. Pi. 2014. "Repeated Strains, Social Control, Social Learning, and Delinquency: Testing and Integrated Model of General Strain Theory in China". *Youth & Society* 46, no. 3: 402–24.

Barona, P., G. Jimenez, and P. Melo. 2019. "Types of Crime, Poverty, Population Density and Presence of Police in the Metropolitan District of Quito". *International Journal of Geo-Information* 8, no. 12: 558. https://doi.org/10.3390/ijgi8120558

Bellair, P. 2017. "Social Disorganisation Theory". *Oxford Research Encyclopedia of Criminology*. https://oxfordre.com/criminology/view/10.1093/acrefore/9780190264079.001.0001/acrefore-9780190264079-e-253 (accessed 24 February 2023).

Carter, A. 2019. "The Consequences of Adolescent Delinquent Behavior for Adult Employment Outcomes". *Journal of Youth and Adolescence* 48: 17–29.

Costello, B. 1997. "On the Logical Adequacy of Cultural Deviance Theories". *Theoretical Criminology* 1, no. 4: 403–28.

Cusinato, M., S. Iannattone, A. Spoto, M. Poli, C. Moretti, M. Gatta, and M. Miscloscia. 2020. "Stress, Resilience, and Well-Being in Italian Children and Their Parents during the COVID-19 Pandemic". *International Journal of Environmental Research and Public Health* 17, no. 22: 8297. https://doi.org/10.3390/ijerph17228297

Duwe, G. 2015. "The Benefits of Keeping Idle Hands Busy: An Outcome Evaluation of a Prisoner Reentry Employment Program". *Crime & Delinquency* 61, no. 4: 559–86.

Fafchamps, M. 2006. "Crime, Transitory Poverty, and Isolation: Evidence from Madagascar". *Economic Development and Cultural Change* 54, no. 3: 579–603. https://doi.org/10.1086/500028

Graif, C., A. Gladfelter, and S. Matthews. 2014. "Urban Poverty and Neighbourhood Effects on Crime: Incorporating Spatial and Network Perspectives". *Sociology Compass* 8, no. 9: 1140–55.

Hawkins, D., and J. Weis. 2015. "The Social Development Model: An Integrated Approach to Delinquency Prevention". In *Developmental and Life-course Criminological Theories*, edited by Paul Mazerolle, pp. 3–28. London: Routledge.

Hay, C., and W. Forrest. 2009. "The Implications of Family for a Pattern of Persistent Offending". In *The Development of Persistent Criminality*, edited by J. Savage, pp. 54–70. Oxford University Press.

Heller, S. 2014. "Summer Jobs Reduce Violence among Disadvantaged Youth". *Science* 346, no. 6214: 1219–23.

Hipp, J., and D. Yates. 2011. "Ghettos, Thresholds, and Crime: Does Concentrated Poverty Really Have an Accelerating Increasing Effect on Crime?". *Criminology* 49, no. 4: 955–90.

Hoffmann, J. 2002. "A Contextual Analysis of Differential Association, Social Control, and Strain Theories of Delinquency". *Social Forces* 81, no. 3: 753–85.

Hooghe, M., B. Vanhoutte, W. Hardyns, and T. Bircan. 2011. "Unemployment, Inequality, Poverty and Crime". *British Journal of Criminology* 51, no. 1: 1–20.

Hsin, A., and C. Felfe. 2014. "When Does Time Matter? Maternal Employment, Children's Time With Parents, and Child Development". *Demography* 51, no. 5: 1867–94.

Huang, C., D. Laing, and P. Wang. 2004. "Crime and Poverty: A Search-Theoretic Approach". *International Economic Review* 45, no. 3: 909–38.

Junger, M., and R. Tremblay. 1999. "Self-Control, Accidents, and Crime". *Criminal Justice and Behaviour* 26, no. 4: 485–501.

Karstedt, S., and B. Kai. 2000. "Introduction: Social Change as a Challenge for Criminological Theory". In *Social Dynamics of Crime and Control: New Theories for a World in Transition*, edited by S. Karstedt and K. Bussmann, pp. 1–10. Hart Publishing.

Kubrin, C., and R. Weitzer. 2003. "New Directions in Social Disorganisation Theory". *Journal of Research in Crime and Delinquency* 40, no. 4: 374–402.

Li, S., T. Liu, and Y. Xia. 2023. "A Comparative Study of Parenting Practices and Juvenile Delinquency between China and the United States". *Deviant Behaviour* 44, no. 4: 636–51.

Matsueda, R. 1997. "Cultural Deviance Theory: The Remarkable Persistence of Flawed Term". *Theoretical Criminology* 1, no. 4: 429–52.

Munabari, F. 2018. "The Quest of Sharia in Indonesia: The Mobilisation Strategy of the Forum of Islamic Society". *Contemporary Islam* 12: 229–49. https://doi.org/10.1007/s11562-018-0416-z

Papaioannou, K. 2007. "'Hunger Makes a Thief of Any Man': Poverty and Crime in British Colonial Asia". *European Review of Economic History* 21, no. 1: 1–28.

Pare, P., and R. Felson. 2014. "Income Inequality, Poverty and Crime across Nations". *British Journal of Sociology* 65, no. 3: 434–58.

Pitt, C., and B. Walker. 2022. "Economic Strain and Adolescent Violence. Are Extracurricular Activities a Conditioning Effect?". *Academicus International Scientific Journal* 25, no. 25: 194–213.

Rogers, E., and Pridemore. 2016. "Research on Social Disorganisation Theory and Crime in Rural Communities". In *The Routledge International Handbook of Rural Criminology*, edited by Joseph Donnermeyer, pp. 23–32. New York: Routledge.

Rukus, J., M. Warner, and X. Zhang. 2018. "Community Policing: Least Effective Where Need Is Greatest". *Crime & Delinquency* 64, no. 14: 1858–81.

Sampson, R., and W. Groves. 1989. "Community Structure and Crime: Testing Social-Disorganisation Theory". *American Journal of Sociology* 94, no. 4: 774–802.

Spruit, A., E. Vugt, C. Put, T. Stouwe, and G. Stams. 2016. "Sports Participation and Juvenile Delinquency: A Meta-Analytic Review". *Journal of Youth and Adolescence* 45: 655–71.

Wadsworth, T. 2000. "Labour Markets, Delinquency, and Social Control Theory: An Empirical Assessment of the Mediating Process". *Social Forces* 78, no. 3: 1041–66.

Warner, B. 2003. "The Role of Attenuated Culture in Social Disorganisation Theory". *Criminology* 41, no. 1: 73–98.

Wiatrowski, M., D. Griswold, and M. Roberts. 1981. "Social Control Theory and Delinquency". *American Sociological Review* 46, no. 5: 525–41.

Wickes, R., J. Hipp, E. Sargeant, and R. Homel. 2013. "Collective Efficacy as a Task-Specific Process: Examining the Relationship Between Social Ties, Neighborhood Cohesion and the Capacity to Respond to Violence, Delinquency and Civic Problems". *American Journal of Community Psychology* 52: 115–27. https://doi.org/10.1007/s10464-013-9582-6

3

Policy Examination of the Socio-economic Root Causes of Sex Work

ABSTRACT

This chapter emphasizes the discussion of the socio-economic construction of prostitution. I rationalize how the encounter of poverty, a lack of informal and formal social control, a lack of positive socialization, peer influence, the existence of cultural deviance and an insufficiency of education opportunities all render disadvantaged Indonesian women and children exposed to a disproportionately high risk of engagement in commercial sex. I, upon unveiling how commercial sex activities are socio-economically constructed and identifying existing relevant socio-economic policy gaps, suggest how disadvantaged populations at higher risks of engaging in commercial sex can be empowered in order to gain a fairer share of opportunities to follow the conventional, legal and morally acceptable route to enter the labour market.

INTRODUCTION

This chapter highlights seven major socio-economic root causes of commercial sex engagement. These are poverty, informal social control, formal social control, a lack of positive socialization, peer influence, cultural deviance and a shortage of education opportunities. The chapter follows by assessing policy development and suggesting policy recommendations that are conducive to mitigating, attenuating and even eradicating these socio-economic root causes of, underage or not, sex work. Understanding the socio-economic root causes of sex work in Indonesian contexts serves as the foundation of the development of Chapter 5, where I will visit Indonesia's anti-extramarital sex law and argue how such criminalization is associated with the country's tolerance of and response to prostitution.

POVERTY

Like other developing Southeast Asian countries, poverty, in both urban and rural forms, has been known as a pressing societal issue that disproportionately affects the vulnerability of people with socio-economic disadvantages in Indonesia (Riswanda, Mills, and Nantes 2017). In this section, I explain how poverty results in the proliferation of prostitution and sex trafficking in Indonesia.

In Indonesia, especially in urban slums and remote, impoverished and rural communities, residents have been subject to significant impacts of poverty (Minnery et al. 2013). Here these residents living in poverty usually face a shortage of basic necessities, including education, food and shelter (Dhanani and Islam 2002; Jones 2017). Their encounters with socio-economic disadvantages make them very vulnerable to being exploited by, for example, sex traffickers, as briefly discussed in the preceding chapters. Indonesian women and children living with socio-economic disadvantages, including poverty, are at high risk of being lured into the sex trade in the hope of securing more life chances and better economic opportunities (Riswanda, Nantes, and Mills 2016). However, unfortunately, they end up being trapped working as modern sex slaves.

Given the socio-economic vulnerability of Indonesian communities living in poverty and Southeast Asia's infamous sex tourism reputation, the problems of prostitution and sex trafficking are perpetuated. Ample people become sex traffickers in order to secure lucrative financial sources and sexual pleasure (i.e., by sexually exploiting sex trafficking victims). They believe, especially in the unregulated underground economy, that exploiting females and children is a channel to satisfy and achieve their own desires and goals. Those who are trafficked into sex work are, in many circumstances, subject to physical, emotional, psychological and sexual abuse. They often are victims of rape and torture (Sutinah and Kinuthia 2019).

Indonesia's institutional loopholes and loose law enforcement and justice systems compound the problems of female and child sexual exploitation. Here law enforcement authorities fail to tightly regulate the commercial sex industry effectively and consistently, allowing ample sex trafficking activities to persistently occur in Indonesia (Dijk 2013). Chapter 4 will focus on addressing the institutional root causes of prostitution and sex trafficking, to further expose how people facing poverty and socio-economic disadvantages can easily be sexually and physically exploited.

Poverty is a pivotal factor that results in prostitution and sex trafficking within the Indonesian context. While the delivery of remedies (such as rescuing sex trafficking victims) and treatment (such as providing psychological counselling services to rescued sex trafficking victims) are important, it is equally necessary for Indonesia to prevent the occurrence of sex work (Manullang 2020). A primary approach is to address and eradicate the socio-economic root causes of prostitution, such as poverty.

INFORMAL SOCIAL CONTROL

As addressed in the preceding chapter, supported by the social control theory, informal and formal social control are important social instruments that can be used to mitigate and discourage people from practising criminality and delinquency. Informal social control refers to any unwritten rules or norms that help regulate people's behaviours and presented traits in society (Groff 2015). Given the informal nature, such social control is not enforced by law but by social pressure to a large degree. In more socially disorganized communities and regions of Indonesia, a shortage of informal social control has resulted in the spike and consolidation of the problem of prostitution and sex trafficking (Scott 2016). Poverty propels the difficulties in forming informal social control. Indonesians may be facing obstacles to supporting their basic amenities, including education, food and housing needs. Poverty, therefore, renders ample poor parents to sell their daughters into the sex trade or hard labour industries in order to gain financial compensation/returns to improve the households' economic conditions (Scott 2016). The experience of, transitory or chronic, poverty has significantly disrupted Indonesian families' everyday life. Parents would practise a lower degree of informal social control, such as sacrificing their social ties with children, by selling their daughters into prostitution (Sutinah and Kinuthia 2019). Such a circumstance indicates how financial well-being may be mitigated at the expense of losing informal social control in Indonesian contexts, prompting women and children living in poverty to provide commercial sex.

In these poor, rural and remote households, children often receive a limited degree of family and community support, contributing to their prevalence of working as prostitutes. Girls who are less protected and connected at the family level are, as per the social control theory, less socially controlled from expressing criminality and delinquency. Especially in more socially disorganized communities, these girls build a lower degree of awareness of complying with conventional, moral and religious norms. They have the disposition to see engagement in sex work as simply an alternative means to survive (Purwanto et al. 2017). The shortage of informal social control such disadvantaged cohorts enjoy makes them evidently vulnerable to sex trafficking. Their encounters with hopelessness, deprivation and isolation all render them to be trapped in the vicious cycle of poverty, prostitution and destitution.

The inadequacy of informal social control in Indonesia, as a result, has prompted an upsurge in prostitution and sex trafficking. Poverty and insufficient family support and social ties aggravate the deep-rooted, long-standing issues of sex work and trafficking (Yulaika 2018). The construction and delivery of a more mature informal social control mechanism have to be realized in the long run in Indonesia should the Indonesian government plan to end the plight of prostitution and sex trafficking and attenuate or tackle the problems of extramarital sex.

Formal Social Control

Like informal social control, formal social control is equally important and needed as a social instrument to help mitigate any form of expression of criminality and delinquency. The levels of formal social control are, in part, determined by the degrees of poverty, law enforcement corruption and the pool of state-level resources. Unless the Indonesian government has the sufficient and necessary resources to investigate and apply police raids to arrest and convict whoever is engaged in prostitution and sex trafficking, such sex crimes will continue to prevail in Indonesia (Cribb 2010). Moreover, the entrenched level of social stigmatization and the taboo against extramarital and premarital sex has engendered the expansion of the underground growth of illegal, commercial sex. When such social stigmatization and the cultural taboo against extramarital sex are not addressed properly, an inflow of prostitutes and sex trafficking victims will continue to enter into the sex trade in the underground economy (Suud 2015). As a result, Indonesia will be subject to a demolished level of formal social control that, in turn, causes the development of commercial sex. Therefore, Chapter 5 will visit the anti-extramarital sex law of Indonesia's parliament and argue how increasingly criminalizing extramarital sex and/or lowering the tolerance of non-marital sex may not necessarily result in a fall in commercial sex incidences. Unless the

Indonesian government can eradicate the root causes of prostitution and sex trafficking, building a lower tolerance of extramarital sex will simply encourage more non-marital sex to occur in the underground, hidden economy.

Women and children coming from impoverished, rural origins may not necessarily have the resources and social and financial security to support their households' everyday needs. These cohorts are often subject to a lack of education and labour market opportunities, rendering them less literate, educated and skilled, and unemployed (with little to no career prospects). These cohorts cannot secure any legitimate means to escape poverty (Susanti et al. 2020). As theorized in the preceding chapter, when people cannot secure sufficiency or any life chances by following legitimate means, they are tempted to, alternatively, express criminality or delinquency as a socio-economic opportunity to help them seek social values and financial gains. These marginalized cohorts are given fewer opportunities to join any community-level or school-level organizations or groups to build their interpersonal relationships and social networks. They are, therefore, less formally and socially controlled from expressing criminality and delinquency.

The shortages of both informal and formal social control have propelled the significant concerns of prostitution and sex trafficking in Indonesia. To curb these issues, the Indonesian government has to allocate more resources to local governing agencies to build up the latter's capacity to combat any form of criminality and delinquency and protect the interests and security of local citizens (Priandika et al. 2020). The more people are socially tied, connected, included and benefited, the more they are controlled from expressing criminality and delinquency.

POSITIVE SOCIALIZATION

Building informal social control is a pivotal part of the delivery of positive socialization. People who are more positively socialized are, simultaneously, more socially controlled. Positive socialization is generically defined as the process where people are given the opportunity to interact with others in a productive, healthy fashion. Positive socialization can be displayed in multiple forms, including the entitlement to family and community support, education and positive role modelling (Sharma 2017). In Indonesia, to a large extent, however, many children and youths are not accessing sufficient opportunities for positive socialization, leaving them vulnerable, to some degree, to both sexual and non-sexual exploitation.

At the family level, child neglect, abandonment and abuse may commonly occur in impoverished, destitute families. Children are given very little to no familial warmth, guidance, supervision or support. Especially if parents send their children into prostitution, these children are deprived of psychological, emotional and social support from their parents that is needed for healthy child development (Riswanda, Mills, and Nantes 2017). According to the social control theory, children and youths who are less positively socialized are prone to displaying a higher tendency to express criminality or delinquency. These underage cohorts follow fewer conventional, moral and religious norms and are more vulnerable to sex work.

At the cultural level, Indonesia, like other neighbouring Southeast Asian countries, contains salient gender inequalities. There are conventional gender roles and expectations that propel domestic families to deem females as commodifiable who can be bought and sold (Farley 2013). In many circumstances, Indonesian women and girls are not given full agency, autonomy and rights, and they are often viewed as subordinate to their male counterparts. In domestic and school settings, these female cohorts are rarely empowered by their parents or teachers to the fullest extent, as women and girls are generally perceived as labour who undertake household chores and, in more extreme circumstances, as commodities to satisfy males' sexual desire (ibid.).

The lack of positive socialization, such as in the forms of poor parenting and gender inequalities, has engendered women and girls to be less socially controlled. While women and girls, per Islamic law, are taught the concepts of how to be well-behaved in public and domestic settings, they, given the continuous gender-based suppression, are facilitated to express criminality and delinquency (Hefner 2019). They are, hence, at high risk of entering the sex industry and providing commercial sex.

PEER INFLUENCE

Another form of informal social control is the level of peer influence. Here I primarily use the social learning theory to justify how negative peer influence prompts Indonesian women and children to enter the sex industry. As addressed, in impoverished and more socially disorganized communities, women and girls are experiencing difficulties in accessing opportunities to form positive social ties (such as with their parents or with teachers). Per the social learning theory, these socially distanced cohorts are inclined to crave interpersonal support and acceptance. They are willing to behave in a way to please their peers, even if such acts are deemed socially undesirable and risky. If peers are providing commercial sex or are drug addicts, these women and girls may end up, under social pressure, to follow and deliver paid sex and/or consume psychoactive substances. Those who become drug addicts are more vulnerable to expressing criminality and delinquency and entering the sex industry as they would need "quick and easy" money to purchase drugs (Wijaya et al. 2018).

Among the delinquent groups, women and girls are easily socially influenced and believe that any form of criminal expression is normalized or, even, socially rewarding. Those who grow up in neighbourhoods or communities where many females are sex trafficked would internalize such an act as socially acceptable and common. To realize assimilation, these women and children may follow their peers and enter the sex industry in order to both earn social rewards and gain financial resources (Wijaya et al. 2018). Especially as these women and children have been systematically and chronically discriminated against and marginalized, they do not have access to sufficient education and labour market opportunities to develop their legitimate social and economic values. They would, therefore, engage in illegitimate activities to earn such social recognition and economic values.

Whoever is socially influenced to express criminality and delinquency is introduced to more opportunities to commit crimes. The social control theory states that when there are accessible opportunities for the expression of criminality and delinquency, people's willingness to act in a deviant manner may be activated. The more social opportunities Indonesian women and children are entitled to enter the sex industry, the more likely they, therefore, will become sex workers. Therefore, Indonesian policymakers have to block access to such opportunities in order to deactivate domestic populations' criminality tendencies or desires.

CULTURAL DEVIANCE

Chapter 2 theorized cultural deviance and explained how such a factor is associated with people's expression of criminality and depression. In this section, I discuss how cultural deviance embedded in Indonesian society propels engagement in commercial sex. In Indonesia or Southeast Asia at large, younger women and girls are, as mentioned, commodified and deemed tradable to richer men in exchange for financial resources (Khanza et al. 2015). Such cultural deviance drives the emergence of sexual predators who target exploiting poverty-stricken households and marginalized groups (such as orphans and street children) by luring them to sell daughters into the sex trade.

Ample impoverished and marginalized Indonesian households see prostitution as a viable income source. While Islamic law significantly condemns any form of commercial sex practice, the historical and socio-cultural contexts of Indonesia have allowed, to some degree, poor domestic families to stay afloat economically by permitting the female members of their households to be sexually exploited. Women and girls who are commodified, given the entrenched cultural deviance and the profound underlying issue of gender inequality, usually share little to no negotiating power to reject any offer of being sexually exploited.

Women and girls, prior to entering into the sex trade, may not necessarily understand fully the dangers and risks of prostitution. They, in many circumstances, only deem entry to the sex industry as a means to earn quick and easy money (Husson 2017). Without realizing the long-term dangers and risks, they become physically and sexually vulnerable once they work as prostitutes. The Indonesian government, however, does not strictly apply laws and regulations to prosecute sexual predators and sex traffickers. Many sex criminals, therefore, operate with impunity to some degree, rendering difficulties in curbing the prevalence of prostitution and sex trafficking.

LACK OF EDUCATION OPPORTUNITIES

Not only does Indonesia lack a well-structured and well-regulated law enforcement system, but the country fails to deliver sufficient education opportunities to Indonesian populations, especially those located in more residentially segregated, financially insecure and socially less engaged and organized communities. The Indonesian government, thus far, does not provide adequate education opportunities to all children, rendering those who are in poverty and have social disadvantages deprived of academic learning and school engagement life chances (Fauk et al. 2018). In the long term, these women and children are, therefore, receiving limited to no opportunities for career advancements or simply stable financial earnings (Dutt 2011). They are, hence, at higher risk of sexual exploitation and being victimized as prostitution and sex trafficking objects.

Without adequate education opportunities, poor Indonesian families send their children to work in low-skilled industries, such as farm work, domestic helping services and/or prostitution. They are deemed naïve, gullible, ignorant about their human and labour rights, and highly exploitable (Ariadne, Pratamawaty, and Limilia 2021; Butt and Munro 2007). Given the socio-cultural and religious unacceptance of prostitution, women and children providing sex work, in most circumstances, enter the underground, informal economy. They are, therefore, receiving little to no protection from the existing law, and their complaints, where applicable, often remain unheard. While Indonesia's parliament tightens its stance against extramarital sex by passing the criminal code on 6 December 2022, the government has to actively and pragmatically protect the rights of domestic, "illegal" and vulnerable sex workers in order to ensure that their development, safety, health and well-being are not completely ignored.

Education is a useful form of cultural resource that helps equip women and children with the necessary and beneficial skills to identify potential risks of expressing criminality and delinquency and to avoid falling prey to exploitative people or circumstances. Education is also an instrument that helps empower disadvantaged women and children to have a higher degree of agency and autonomy to determine their own lives, futures and rights. So long as they are more educated, they are more literate and skilled and, thus, are more favourable in the labour market (Riswanda et al. 2017). They are, hence, given more life chances to uplift their socio-economic well-being and prevent themselves from being sexually and physically exploited.

Policy Examination of Curbing Poverty

The prevalence of commercial sex and the unequal power of relations underneath that discriminates against women and children of disadvantaged status, has resulted in systematic exploitation against vulnerable cohorts. In order to address any human rights concerns that are violated and to protect the physical, psychological and sexual health of people subjected to socio-economic disadvantages, in the following sections, I examine the needed policy development to help address the aforementioned root causes of sex work. In the preceding chapter, I noted that I am addressing pro-poor interventions that are necessary to curb poverty and poverty-driven prostitution. I, hereby, present how relevant pro-poor interventions can be constructed.

To address poverty-led commercial sex, local governing agencies of Indonesia have to ensure that they provide sufficient basic amenities to the domestic, impoverished populations. These amenities include basic healthcare services, shelter and food. Such an intervention helps socially protect the subsistence needs of disadvantaged populations, in addition to disincentivizing them from engaging in commercial sex. To further socially include and protect underprivileged women and children, the Indonesian government should actively arrange the formation of public-private initiatives, in order to deliver education, vocational training and on-the-job training programmes to underprivileged cohorts to help these beneficiaries gain more educational credentials and skills that are favourable in Indonesia's labour market under the subsidies provided by the public sector. The more skills and education levels women and girls enjoy, the more likely they can secure wage labour positions and, even, develop career prospects and become self-sufficient to support their households in the long run.

While disincentivizing underprivileged cohorts from being sexually exploited is important, it is equally crucial for the Indonesian government to eradicate the channels for prostitution and sex trafficking. The more available sources for commercial sex in Indonesia experience, the more sex crime groups will continue luring and tricking underprivileged women and girls into being sex trafficked. Therefore, lowering the sources and channels for the sexual transaction are both equally needed. It is pragmatically infeasible to completely eliminate the demand for commercial sex, but the Indonesian government can increase the costs of buying sex in order to disincentivize the popularity of sex work. Here the Indonesian government has to actively target the investigation of sex trafficking and prostitution rings, as well as aggressively prosecute those who are engaged in commercial sex. More punitive terms have to be applied against arrested and convicted sex crime offenders, in order to deter more people from initiating or operating the involvement of sexual transactions. Disincentivizing women and girls to enter the sex industry helps lower the supply of prostitution. Simultaneously, applying more punitive terms against those involved in organizing sex trafficking and prostitution activities helps reduce the support for prostitution too. When higher costs are bound to the supply of commercial sex, the prices sexual clients have to pay increase and the available, accessible channels such customers can reach out to commercial sex services attenuate. In sum, the demand for commercial sex will drop in phases.

To further disincentivize women and children from being sexually exploited, initiating community engagement is prominent. Per the social disorganization theory, as discussed in the preceding chapter, local governing agencies and community groups/leaders should cooperate and communicate closely in order to build domestic populations' awareness of avoiding the expression of criminality and delinquency by complying strictly with conventional, religious, social and moral values. Here more community-level programmes should be organized and made available to all domestic residents to educate them on how to prevent themselves or their families from being sexually and physically exploited, as well as highlighting the importance for them to report suspected criminal activities or delinquencies to local law enforcement authorities. Such a form of community policing helps enhance anti-crime awareness at the community level, minimizing the opportunities for sex traffickers and conventional sex establishment owners to recruit vulnerable cohorts to be physically, sexually, psychologically and financially exploited. Moreover, promoting the practice of community policing helps discourage women and children from voluntarily entering the sex industry for financial gains. With the presence of community policing, those working as voluntary sex workers with full consent bear higher costs and more risks for their provision of commercial sex services. Therefore, they are less likely to enter the sex industry either on a full-time, part-time or freelance basis. With a minimized supply of commercial sex, the Indonesian government can heighten the intensity of its crackdowns on extramarital sex. While causal sex—where money is not involved—may not be addressed, those violating anti-extramarital sex law by finding prostitution services can be discouraged from continuing with their sexual misconduct that breaches the moral and religious values outlined in Islamic law.

POLICY EXAMINATION OF STRENGTHENING (IN-)FORMAL SOCIAL CONTROL

Indonesia, like other Southeast Asian countries, has to build a more socially tied and connected society. Indonesia is able to benefit from the enjoyment of higher social cohesion and more favourable economic conditions, so long as its populations are more socially engaged and connected. Therefore, the Indonesian government has to actively strengthen the levels of (in-)formal social control that is conducive to harness people from expressing criminality and delinquency.

Community-based organizations, such as civil society organizations and religious institutions, play an important role in promoting social norms that support the well-being, stability and prosperity of communities. These community-based organizations should actively advocate the importance of following moral values that Islamic law upholds in order to build awareness of self-discipline (Hashim and Langgulung 2008). Sexual ethics, especially on females, are popularly promoted in Islam. Here female virginity, for example, remains an important aspect determining the future of women and girls. Despite the presence of sexual ethics, cases of rape, sexual violence and sex slavery have been an ongoing issue in the Islamic world which reflects the broader societal and cultural problems of gender inequality, female objectification and male dominance (Ali 2016 [2006]). Such community-based organizations should, concurrently, organize more health and safety information-sharing sessions. Here professionals and community leaders should inform the general public about the dangers and risks women and girls being sexually traded are subject to, in addition to how such vulnerable cohorts can better protect their own interests (such as tactics to negotiate the performance of safe sex) if they are unfortunately to be sex trafficked.

Empowering local residents to report cases of prostitution and sex trafficking is, as indicated in the preceding section, a needed approach to building the levels of social control the general public possesses. It is noteworthy that residents are less motivated to report any cases of misconduct, crime or delinquency if the levels of social trust within communities or towards law enforcement authorities are low (Cameron and Shah 2014). Therefore, community-based organizations have to actively operate within villages and cities by hosting more public information sessions and social and recreational activities that allow local residents to build levels of trust towards their belonging communities. Moreover, Chapter 4 will delineate how police corruption has to be addressed and how the loose justice system has to be reformed. By building a more effective, respectful law enforcement mechanism, residents shall enjoy a higher level of trust towards law enforcement authorities and institutions. As a result, they are more motivated to report any case of deviance and criminality. Law enforcement authorities have to ensure that anonymity and confidentiality are guaranteed when reporting any suspicious cases, otherwise, domestic residents would not be incentivized to fulfil their social responsibilities.

Community-based organizations should host more economic empowerment programmes too. Very often, women and children coming from impoverished, rural and poor origins are at high risk of being victimized by prostitution and sex trafficking. Community-based organizations, therefore, have to provide such underprivileged cohorts with the opportunities to learn valuable vocational skills and even collaborate with local businesses to create job vacancies. The more job opportunities communities provide, and the more skills development opportunities underprivileged cohorts can gain access to, the less likely they would end up entering the sex industry.

Furthermore, to curb commercial sex and sex trafficking, the Indonesian government has to ensure that a comprehensive, concrete legal framework to prohibit and sanction organized sex crimes is in place. The Indonesian government has to consider partnering with local NGOs and other civil organizations to deliver awareness-building and training programmes for judicial officers, law enforcement authorities and the general public on how each actor should respond to any form of sexual exploitation or violence. The Indonesian government has to deliver more funding to local governing agencies to ensure that the local government units have sufficient financial capacity to arrange and deliver these programmes to avoid sexual exploitation and curb prostitution in the long run.

The Indonesian government has to acknowledge the importance of responding to the encounters with the root causes of prostitution, namely poverty and inequality. In addition to the provision of education and vocational training opportunities, the Indonesian government and local governing agencies have to provide financial assistance designated for low-income, unemployed and/or disabled cohorts. While the provision of temporary financial relief does not help empower the underprivileged cohorts in the long term, such a social protection policy is important to deter impoverished women and children from considering entry into the sex industry.

Local governing agencies should, moreover, collaborate with domestic healthcare institutions to provide rehabilitation services and therapeutic care to whoever is being rescued from prostitution and sex trafficking. Moreover, voluntary sex workers who intend to leave the sex industry may also need such healthcare support as victims of prostitution and sex trafficking are vulnerable to the experience of constant violence, abuse and exploitation (Lyneham and Larsen 2013).

Fighting against commercial sex and human trafficking in Indonesia requires the employment of a multi-dimensional approach that, in part, involves the application and consolidation of both formal and informal social control. With the presence of higher levels of social control, Indonesia will be able to create a higher degree of social stability, a lower level of fear of crime, a less interpersonally-tensioned living environment, and a society with more favourable economic conditions that attract foreign or local investments—as a result, more job opportunities will be created within the country.

POLICY EXAMINATION OF PROMOTING POSITIVE
SOCIALIZATION

To further address socio-economically-led commercial sex engagement, the Indonesian government has to enrich its social welfare programme that prioritizes poverty reduction. While social protection schemes are designated for underprivileged cohorts, poor populations living in the most remote, least developed and rural villages often find such welfare and benefits inaccessible. Indonesia has to ensure that social protection schemes are reachable to regions that are infamous for the provision of sex workers. Specifically empowering women and children from those regions helps mitigate the levels of socio-economic disadvantages and deprivation underprivileged cohorts are subject to in order to disincentivize them from entering the sex industry.

Community-based organizations have to, simultaneously, deliver more public education seminars and workshops for parents of impoverished households. Here parents should be educated on how to build their awareness of protecting the interests of their children, regardless of sex. Moreover, parents should be taught the social and psychological support they can use on their children if the latter is identified as being sexually exploited or abused. Teaching less-literate parents the importance of applying apt parenting approaches and demonstrating parental warmth is pivotal to preventing women and children from being sexually exploited in the long term.

In a broader context, Indonesia has to actively challenge the ingrained gender inequality and cultural normalization of sex work. As a status quo, females, especially those who are in a disadvantaged position, are commodified and made available in the sex trade market. The Indonesian government, local governing agencies and community-based organizations have to collectively challenge the involved problem of gender inequality where females within Indonesian society are often deemed subordinate. Concurrently, more education and job opportunities have to be made accessible to both males and females, allowing women and girls to receive a fairer share of life chances and develop their own career prospects and strengths. The more disincentivized these empowered female cohorts are from entering the sex industry, the less likely they will work as sex labourers. Empowering females is one of the most direct and effective channels to attenuate the levels of cultural normalization of sex work. As a consequence, Indonesia can challenge the socio-cultural structure that discriminates against female cohorts and prompts them to engage in commercial sex. Ultimately, any successful and effective approaches towards curbing prostitution and sex trafficking require a fundamental shift of the mindset of Indonesian populations, in order to encourage the practice of positive socialization that bars underprivileged cohorts from expressing criminality or delinquency.

POLICY EXAMINATION OF PROMOTING POSITIVE PEER INFLUENCE

As much as the culture of presenting positive socialization should be sharpened, Indonesia cannot overlook the importance of addressing any form of negative peer influence. Cultivating positive peer influences where ethical and moral values are shared is necessary for Indonesia to prevent women and children from entering the sex trade market. Community-based organizations have to, as mentioned, create and organize regular social, educational and recreational events for local residents to attend. These events include peer support groups and mentorship initiatives where residents are given a favourable environment to mutually support the moral beliefs and practices of one another, alongside brainstorming solutions to tackle any socio-economic challenges each of them faces in a legitimate, sustainable and safe manner. Beneficiaries of these initiatives can be socially empowered and influenced to be well-behaved and follow the social, cultural, religious and legal norms of avoiding any sexual misconduct, for example.

The Indonesian government should actively engage in capacity building for law enforcement and justice agencies to help such institutions sufficiently investigate and prosecute whoever is involved in prostitution and sex trafficking. For example, perpetrators of these crimes should be sanctioned severely. The more punitive terms Indonesia's law enforcement agencies apply, the more disincentivized these perpetrators become from attempting to socially connect with underprivileged cohorts to take advantage of their socio-economic disadvantages, bodies and/or ignorance.

Peer influence is neutral. The Indonesian government has to actively minimize the circulation of negative peer influences within local communities and heighten the collective promotion of positive peer influences. Peer influences, if properly arranged, can help Indonesia curb prostitution and sex trafficking, as underprivileged cohorts are more socially harnessed from expressing criminality and delinquency.

POLICY EXAMINATION OF ATTENUATING CULTURAL DEVIANCE

Indonesia has, moreover, to champion the morally, religiously and socially rightful values that prohibit sex work and trafficking. Schools and community-based organizations have to serve as the primary institutions to deliver education programmes that focus on teaching beneficiaries the moral values and social responsibilities Indonesian nations should comply. The Indonesian government or local governing agencies can partner with NGOs to provide information sessions to the general public on promoting healthy sexual behaviours, compliance with appropriate sexual conduct and the need to perform safe sex.

Tightening the law enforcement efforts against any form of extramarital sex, including commercial sex, allows the general public to understand and be aware of how wrongful and risky sexual misconduct is per Islamic law and Indonesian contexts at large. Heavily criminalizing the engagement in commercial sex helps emphasize how deviant the culture of sex work is. Therefore, law enforcement authorities have to vigorously arrest, investigate, interrogate and prosecute whoever is involved in commercial sex, as a presentation of the prohibition of such cultural deviance in Indonesian contexts.

To tighten law enforcement against sex work, Indonesian authorities should incorporate technologies to address such cultural deviance. As prostitution and sex trafficking in Southeast Asia are increasingly digitalized, the Indonesian government has to set up digital crime teams that are primarily or exclusively responsible for monitoring commercial sex-related criminal activities on the Internet. Suspicious Internet users should be arrested for interrogation and potentially for prosecution. Indonesia, along with neighbouring, developing Southeast Asian countries, has a lack of e-regulation on cybercrimes (Awaludin 2019). Tightening up the e-regulations is essentially pivotal not only because the growth of organized crime has been digitalized, but also because there are more regulatory loopholes on the Internet than in any social settings that deepen women and children's vulnerability when they are online.

POLICY EXAMINATION OF PROMOTING EDUCATIONAL DEVELOPMENT

On multiple occasions in this book, I reiterate how education, vocational training and on-the-job training opportunities have to be distributed to Indonesian nationals countrywide. Education is a crucial part when eradicating any form of sexual exploitation, as intellectual and awareness empowerment is conducive to the development of Indonesian women and children's critical thinking, independent thinking and problem-solving skills. More empowered people are, moreover, understanding their rights as human, Indonesian citizens or as Muslims. Therefore, the provision of education is beneficial to strengthening people's opportunities to protect their safety, health and well-being concerns.

The Indonesian government and local governing agencies have to invest more in the education sector to raise the amount of urban and especially rural schools as much as attenuate the financial burdens that bar underprivileged school-aged students from receiving education. More merit-based and especially need-based financial support in the forms of scholarships, grants, subsidies and loans have to be made available in the public education sector, allowing students, specifically girls, from poor, rural households to be able to attend school. In the long run, education universalization helps enhance the levels of human investment and development enjoyed in Indonesia which is conducive to the country's endeavours to curb poverty and commercial sex prevalence.

Not only should students be educated about intellectual knowledge and vocational skills at schools, but they should be given opportunities to receive sex education. Sex education has to be integrated into the school curriculum in order to empower students with the necessary knowledge and awareness of complying with appropriate sexual conduct and avoiding being sexually exploited. Sex education can also inform school-aged children about how to form healthy relationships and how important consent is when performing sexual or non-sexual relationships. The more knowledgeable students become in sexual conduct, the more positive attitudes they will have towards sex and the more unlikely they will be lured into prostitution and unwanted/unintended (early) pregnancies.

Educational interventions should, additional, encompass the delivery of life-skill development opportunities. Here school-aged students should be able to learn different vocational skills like baking, jewellery making and tailoring that are practical to help them secure a source of wage/income/ revenue. So long as undereducated cohorts are able to earn a living without the need to engage in prostitution, they will be self-sufficient and are less likely to express criminality and delinquency.

Education is, therefore, a cultural and human asset that is so valuable to the extent that better-educated cohorts can be socio-economically, occupationally and sexually empowered and protected to a large degree.

Underprivileged cohorts, including girls, who are entitled to a variety of educational opportunities are less likely to engage in the sex industry or perform any form of misconduct at large.

Conclusion

In Indonesia, engagement in sex work is significantly socio-economically constructed. The more socio-economic disadvantages and deprivation women and children are subject to, the less likely they live up to the conventional, moral, social, religious and legal norms/values that they used to practise. Also, the more disadvantaged they are, the more driving factors they will encounter that tempt them to enter the sex industry. Those who are trapped in prostitution are vulnerable to physical, social, sexual and psychological health and well-being. The longer time they remain in the sex industry, the more segregated and detached they become from the conventional labour market and society as a whole. Therefore, these cohorts may permanently stay in the sex industry until their sex market values completely depreciate to a non-favourable level. The prevention of extramarital sex is not only to satisfy Muslims' need to comply with Islamic law, but also to help underprivileged cohorts within the unequal power of relations in Indonesian society avoid facing any sex-related form of exploitation. The criminalization of extramarital sex practised by the Indonesian government can, therefore, in part, deem Indonesia's stance of lowering the tolerance of sexual exploitation against people facing socio-economic disadvantages.

References

Ali, K. 2016 [2006]. *Sexual Ethics And Islam: Feminist Reflections on Qur'an, Hadith, and Jurisprudence*. London: Oneworld Publications.

Ariadne, E., B. Pratamawaty, and P. Limilia. 2021. "Human Trafficking in Indonesia: The Dialectic of Poverty and Corruption". *Jurnal Hmu-ilmu Sosial dan Humaniora* 23, no. 3: 356–63.

Awaludin, A. 2019. "The Uncertainty of Regulating Online Prostitution in Indonesia". *Proceedings of the 3rd International Conference on Globalisation of Law and Local Wisdom* (ICGLOW 2019). https://doi.org/10.2991/icglow-19.2019.81

Butt, L., and J. Munro. 2007. "Rebel Girls? Unplanned Pregnancy and Colonialism in Highlands Papua, Indonesia". *Culture, Health & Sexuality* 9, no. 6: 585–98.

Cameron, L., and M. Shah. 2014. "Can Mistargeting Destroy Social Capital and Stimulate Crime? Evidence from a Cash Transfer Programme in Indonesia". *Economic Development and Cultural Change* 62, no. 2: 1–44.

Cribb, R. 2010. "A System of Exemptions: Historicising State Illegality in Indonesia".

In *The State and Illegality in Indonesia*, edited by V. Taal and L. Volkenkunde, pp. 29–44. London: Brill.

Dhanani, S., and I. Islam. 2002. "Poverty, Vulnerability and Social Protection in a Period of Crisis: The Case of Indonesia". *World Development* 30, no. 7: 1211–31.

Dijk, K. 2013. *Regime Change, Democracy and Islam: The Case of Indonesia—Final Report Islam Research Programme Jakarta March 2013*. Leiden: Universiteit Leiden.

Dutt, K. 2011. *Gendering the Field: Towards Sustainable Livelihoods for Mining Communities*. Canberra: Griffin Press.

Farley, M. 2013. "Prostitution, Liberalism, and Slavery". *Logos: A Journal of Modern Society & Culture*. https://prostitutionresearch.com/prostitution-liberalism-and-slavery/ (accessed 6 March 2023).

Fauk, N., C. Kustanti, R. Wulandari, A. Damayani, and L. Mwanri. 2018. "Societal Determinants of HIV Vulnerability among Clients of Female Commercial Sex Workers in Indonesia". *PLoS ONE* 13, no. 11: e0207647. https://doi.org/10.1371/journal.pone.0207647

Groff, E. 2015. "Informal Social Control and Crime Events". *Journal of Contemporary Criminal Justice* 31, no. 1: 90–106.

Hashim, C., and H. Langgulung. 2008. "Islamic Religious Curriculum in Muslim Countries: The Experiences of Indonesia and Malaysia". *Bulletin of Education & Research* 30, no. 1: 1–19.

Hefner, C. 2019. "On Fun and Freedom: Young Women's Moral Learning in Indonesian Islamic Boarding Schools". *Journal of the Royal Anthropological Institute* 25, no. 3: 487–505.

Husson, L. 2017. "Who Are the Clients and What They Say About Prostitution in South-East Asia?". *Moussons* 29: 209–62. https://doi.org/10.4000/moussons.3805

Jones, P. 2017. "Formalizing the Informal: Understanding the Position of Informal Settlements and Slums in Sustainable Urbanization Policies and Strategies in Bandung, Indonesia". *Sustainability* 9, no. 8: 1436. https://doi.org/10.3390/su9081436

Khanza, C., O. Yuvia, I. Rezki, and U. Mada. 2015. "Prostitution and. Women Empowerment's Role". *Journal of Business on Hospitality and Tourism* 1, no. 1: 1–9.

Lyneham, S., and J. Larsen. 2013. "Exploitation of Indonesian Trafficked Men, Women and Children and Implications for Support". *Trends and Issues in Crime and Criminal Justice* 450: 1–7.

Manullang, S. 2020. "The Online Prostitution Act from Legal Sociology Perspective in Indonesia". *International Research Journal of Management, IT & Social Sciences* 7, no. 4: 36–42.

Minnery, J., T. Argo, H. Winarso, D. Hau, C. Veneracion, D. Forbes, and I. Childs. 2013. "Slum Upgrading and Urban Governance: Case Studies in Three South East Asian Cities". *Habitat International* 39: 162–69. https://doi.org/10.1016/j.habitatint.2012.12.002

Priandika, J., E. Pandu, M. Mualip, and R. Setiawan. 2020. "Prostitution, Crime, and

Law Enforcement: Criminology Studies in the Argorejo Resocialisation and Rehabilitation and Semarang City". *Law Research Review Quarterly* 6, no. 3: 247–64.

Purwanto, E., D. Kameo, J. Ihalauw, and S. Priyanto. 2017. "The Complexity of Poverty among Benteng Chinese in Tangerang District, Indonesia". *Journal of Applied Economic Sciences* 3, no. 49: 820–31.

Riswanda, R., Y. Nantes, and J. Mills. 2016. "Re-Framing Prostitution in Indonesia: A Critical Systemic Approach". *Systemic Practice and Action Research* 29: 517–39. https://doi.org/10.1007/s11213-016-9379-2

———, J. Mills, and Y. Nantes. 2017. "Prostitution and Human Rights in Indonesia: A Critical Systemic Review of Policy Discourses and Scenarios". *Systemic Practice and Action Research* 30: 213–17. https://doi.org/10.1007/s11213-016-9393-4

Scott, J. 2016. "Rural Prostitution". In *The Routledge International Handbook of Rural Criminology*, edited by J. Donnermeyer, pp. 75–84. London: Routledge.

Sharma, A. 2017. "Learning and Consumer Socialisation in Children". In *Young Consumer Behaviour*, edited by A. Gbadamosi, pp. 57–78. London: Routledge.

Susanti, V., M. Kosandi, N. Subono, and E. Kartini. 2020. "Criminological Study on Criminal Activities Human Trafficking in the Nusa Tenggara Timur Region (NTT), Indonesia". *International Journal of Criminology and Sociology* 9, no. 1: 182–91.

Sutinah, S., and K. Kinuthia. 2019. "Trafficking of Women and Children in East Java, Indonesia". *Journal of International Women's Studies* 20, no. 9: Article 9. https://vc.bridgew.edu/jiws/vol20/iss9/9

Suud, M. 2015. "Appropriate Policy on Prostitution in Indonesia: A Strategy to Minimise Social Impacts in Society". *Public Policy and Administration Research* 5, no. 10: 96–110.

Wijaya, I., M. Giri, N. Wahyuni, and K. Setiawan. 2018. "Premarital Sex Behaviours of Teenagers: A Case in Bali, Indonesia". *International Journal of Health Sciences* 2, no. 3: 11–21.

Yulaika, N. 2018. "Social Capital of Indonesia and Its Development". *IOSR Journal of Humanities and Social Science* 23, no. 8: 51–57.

Policy Examination of the Institutional Root Causes of Sex Work

ABSTRACT

This chapter emphasizes the discourse on the institutional construction of prostitution. I rationalize how institutional barriers to compliance with morality have to be addressed. These institutional barriers include bad governance, a weak law enforcement system, and the practice of corruption. I argue how the existence and prevalence of these institutional barriers worsen the socio-economic difficulties faced by those living in poverty and encourage the commitment to crimes, including entry into the sex industry. Upon unveiling how commercial sex activities are institutionally constructed and identifying existing, relevant institutional policy gaps, I suggest how disadvantaged populations at higher risks of engaging in commercial sex can be institutionally intervened and barred from the expression of immorality and delinquency. As a result, those who intend to work, or are already working, in the sex industry are hampered by engagement in sexual transactions.

INTRODUCTION

Addressing the socio-economic root causes of prostitution is essential, as such an approach helps disincentivize Indonesian women and girls from entering the sex industry. However, if there are significant institutional loopholes when governing people's behaviours, disciplines and morality (such as the discussion of the lack of e-regulation on the Internet to crack down on cyber-sex crime), organized sex crime groups can continue to exploit the loose regulatory, legislative, judiciary and law enforcement mechanism to arrange and deliver sex trafficking and prostitution activities (Awaludin 2019). Therefore, this chapter, in order to minimize Indonesian nationals' violation of anti-extramarital sex, or specifically commercial sex, discusses how commercial sex is institutionally constructed. I then examine the relevant policies to understand how the formation of the institutional mechanism against sex work can be strengthened.

POOR GOVERNANCE, POVERTY AND SEX WORK

Indonesia ranks 130th in the globe, per the Human Development Index, indicating that poverty and inequalities are salient within the country (Antara News 2022). Thus far, this book examines and discusses how poverty, inequalities, a lack of human investment in the form of the distribution of education opportunities and engagement in sex work are interrelated. A primary reason leading to Indonesia's poor human development is the poor governance of the Indonesian government. The formation, implementation and evaluation of policies are crucial parts that define the growth and development of a country. With the absence or shortage of a strong, efficient, effective and consistent policy formation, implementation and evaluation system, governments fail to deliver positively impactful policies and interventions that help attenuate poverty and inequalities (Arifin et al. 2015). In Indonesia, policymakers have not maximized their focus on applying social welfare interventions that are conducive to improving underprivileged cohorts' well-being and development. As a consequence, Indonesia has experienced deepened poverty, inequalities and unemployment, leaving the socio-economic status of some portions of Indonesian nationals unchecked.

The deviant culture of law enforcement corruption is another vital issue that has been plaguing Indonesia's efficiency and effectiveness in governance (Arifin et al. 2015). According to the 2022 survey conducted by IndexMundi, Indonesia's police force was the eighteenth most corrupt in the globe. Also, the Indonesian police force is the most corrupt among Southeast Asian countries (Ramli 2022). Alternatively, the annual Corruption Perceptions Index focuses on ranking corruption in relation to business risks, climate change and others. Among 180 countries that are examined, Indonesia ranks as low as 110th with a score of 34 which implies Indonesia is highly corrupt (Transparency International 2023). With the entrenched presence of corruption, national resources, welfare and benefits cannot be fairly equally distributed to Indonesian nationals, where those belonging to underprivileged socio-economic status are deprived of being socially protected. The public funds that are supposed to be used for national and local development and/or social protection scheme initiation and implementation may be financially exploited by corrupt Indonesian officials. Without addressing the deep-rooted issue of corruption within Indonesia's governing system, those in power continue to exploit the interests of the national population, including those facing socio-economic disadvantages (Dick and Mulholland 2016). Ample underprivileged cohorts will, as a result, continue to be placed in a position with little to no social protection and inclusion.

Indonesia has lacked robust institutions in the forms of parliament, judiciary and law enforcement agencies compounding the levels of poor governance of the country. These institutions are the backbone of any strong, functional governance system. As a status quo, Indonesian institutions have been plagued with issues that include weak oversight, a lack of independence and low transparency (Dick and Mulholland 2016). These circumstances have given room for corruption and governmental misconduct. Indonesian nationals, therefore, develop a lack of trust towards their government (Davies, Stone, and Buttle 2016). As discussed in the preceding chapter, the Indonesian population's lack of trust towards the government bars the Indonesian government from building communities with a low tolerance for criminality and delinquency. As a result, with the shortage of trust towards the government, Indonesia's problems of local crime rates, in addition to national poverty and poor socio-economic conditions, persist.

Poor governance has, in the contexts within and beyond Indonesia, been significantly contributing to the exacerbation of poverty, socio-economic disadvantages and crime rates. Unless the Indonesian government can actively address the weak, ineffective and inconsistent policies, political corruption and loose institutional mechanisms, otherwise the government will continue to face substantial obstacles to realizing national progress (Dick and Mulholland 2016). To strengthen the national institutional mechanism, transparency and accountability in governance must be tightly incorporated (Sofyani, Pratolo, and Saleh 2022). So long as the issues of chronic poverty and socio-economic disadvantages are better addressed, Indonesia can, to some degree, deconstruct the socio-economic drivers of the expression of criminality and delinquency.

It is noteworthy that the prevalence of child prostitution and sex trafficking in Indonesia reflects the insufficient protection of children's rights within the country. Despite passing the 2002 Law on Child Protection, child sex work and sex trafficking remain thriving domestically, showing that the law enforcement system is saliently weak and fragmented (Jauhari 2014). Here Indonesian policymakers have an inadequate level of political will and commitment to eradicate the problems of child sexual exploitation, in which ample government officials are involved in the sex trade of children. When government officials engage in committing child sex trafficking themselves, the Indonesian government and local governing agencies are disincentivized from eradicating child prostitution and trafficking otherwise the interests of those in power would be harmed. The structural problems of poor governance cannot be addressed overnight. An internal investigation, interrogation and prosecution against government officials who are involved in the trafficking of children can only be accomplished if the Indonesian government strategically raises the levels of transparency and accountability in its governance in the long run (Sofyani, Pratolo, and Saleh 2022). Here clearer socio-legal frameworks have to be established in which the Indonesian government should present a firm and clear stance on how governmental officials who are involved in sex trafficking and corruption would be significantly sanctioned. Tightening law enforcement efforts have to be incorporated in order to ensure that the socio-legal framework is more than rhetoric. By holding government officials accountable, government officials will understand that they cannot act with impunity and that they have to pay for their criminal or delinquent acts.

When addressing the poor governance of Indonesia, the country has to ensure that socio-economic empowerment in favour of the interests of domestic citizens is in place too. This is because persistent, chronic socio-economic disadvantages are drivers of poor governance of the Indonesian government. When Indonesia continually experiences poverty and socio-economic insecurity and inequality, an institutionally fertile ground for, underage or not, sexual exploitation is created. This is because government officials and law enforcement authorities are given access to criminal opportunities as they are aware of the socio-economic benefits they can gain by exploiting the interests of the already underprivileged women and children. According to the social control theory, should there be opportunities to commit a crime, people are inclined to express their criminality and delinquency in order to, for example, secure economic returns. Only by socio-economically empowering the underprivileged cohorts in poor Indonesian regions, local governing agencies and their government officials are given less access to opportunities for financially and sexually exploiting women and children. As a result, the Indonesian government will face fewer obstacles to encountering the problems of poor governance.

The Indonesian public, to date, may not necessarily have an awareness of the problems of sex trafficking and prostitution, as such behaviours may be culturally normalized and legally less regulated in some localities (Riswanda 2015). Also, they may fear retaliation if they report any case of sex trafficking and sexual exploitation. With the lack of a community-level sense of belonging and social obligations, the Indonesian public may be prone to turn a blind eye to any sexual misconduct or sex crimes. Indonesian government officials, therefore, have the responsibility to strengthen their social ties and relationships with domestic citizens. Only by building a heightened degree of trust towards the local governing agencies can the Indonesian public learn the importance of fulfilling their social obligations and report any suspicious cases of possible sex crimes to local authorities, allowing Indonesia to consolidate its quality and effectiveness of governance. Breaking the silence surrounding prostitution and sex trafficking, hence, is necessary to improve Indonesia's governance, community organization and law enforcement against any acts of sexual misconduct that breach Indonesia's laws or Islamic laws.

LAW ENFORCEMENT SYSTEM, POVERTY AND SEX WORK

Poor governance and weak law enforcement mechanisms are intertwined to a large degree. Indonesia demonstrates its loose law enforcement system by exposing its problem of political and law enforcement corruption (Sofyani, Pratolo, and Saleh 2022). As addressed briefly above, the issues of corruption have disrupted Indonesia's delivery of public services, access to basic needs (such as education, healthcare and housing) and infrastructure development. As an output of the weak law enforcement system, Indonesia has resulted in a prevalence of crime, including illegal sexual activities, nationwide. Indonesian nationals, especially those living in less socially organized communities, are barred from developing a sense of security, protecting their properties, enjoying favourable economic conditions and opportunities, and building social trust and cohesion. These circumstances, in turn, worsen the degree of social disorganization in Indonesia, prompting the exacerbation of the expression of criminality and delinquency. Fewer domestic and foreign investments would be made in more impoverished, less regulated and socially more disorganized communities, hindering the local economic growth and causing the surge of poverty-led crime, including sex work.

Not only does a weak, ineffective law enforcement system fail to prevent women and children from entering the sex industry or to rescue them to leave prostitution, but such an institutional loophole is compounding the degrees of socio-economic disadvantages suffered by Indonesian populations. As a result, more women and children may be put in a socio-economically vulnerable position where they have to enter into the sex trade to seek subsistence resources. A highlight is the heightened difficulty for disadvantaged populations to gain access to essential public resources, if their belonging localities own a weak law enforcement system. When more underprivileged cohorts are not protected, they are deemed to be ignored by whoever is in power. Once these underprivileged cohorts express criminality and delinquency their poverty-stricken victimizations would be overlooked unless such circumstances are harming the interests of others of more socio-economic privileges.

So long as the law enforcement system in Indonesia is weak, national poverty and socio-economic disadvantages occur persistently and in multi-faceted dimensions (Riswanda, Nantes, and Mills 2016). With unaddressed issues of corruption and crime, Indonesia's economic growth and sustainable development are significantly costed. Again, such an expected outcome illustrates why the Indonesian government should fulfil its responsibilities to raise the transparency and accountability of governance, so as to facilitate the amendment or construction of an effective, healthy, well-facilitated law enforcement system.

Indonesia lacks adequate laws and regulations to specifically protect minors from being sexually exploited. Despite the presence of relevant legalization, the laws are weakly, loosely and inconsistently enforced, allowing ample minors to continue being sexually exploited and abused (Riswanda, Nantes, and Mills 2016). In addition, there is an absence of a consistent, nationally representative database that enables tracking the occurrence of, child or adult, sex trafficking, hindering the Indonesian government and its local law enforcement agencies from identifying, arresting and sanctioning those who are involved in sex crimes (Nuraeny 2017).

Indonesia's encounters with poverty and weak economy contribute to the prevalence of prostitution and sex trafficking. Women and children remain engaging in prostitution out of desperation and facing the need to support their households financially. Without tightly and consistently enforcing the laws to disrupt pimp and trafficking networks, more women and children would be trapped in sexual exploitation, poverty and health risks. Corruption is a factor that results in the slow processing and sentencing of sex traffickers and pimps, enabling many who are involved in sex crimes to continue operating their illegal businesses with some degree of impunity (Sofyani, Pratolo, and Saleh 2022).

Indonesia has to take a stronger stance concerning the enforcement of laws and regulations where measures to protect women and children from sexual exploitation have to be implemented. The country has to address the root causes of commercial sex, in which, as discussed, the socio-economic and institutional drivers of prostitution are intertwined. Only with a stronger, more effective and more consistent law enforcement system can Indonesia promote a safer, healthier living and working environment for all nationals, regardless of their socio-economic status.

POLICE CORRUPTION, POVERTY AND SEX WORK

Multiple times, I illustrate the problem of police, or law enforcement, at large, corruption and how such a problem affects Indonesia's construction of commercial sex. In this section, I focus on addressing the nuanced relationships between police corruption, poverty, socio-economic disadvantages and sex work.

I reiterate that police corruption siphons public resources, making the already economically less developed economy more vulnerable to the encounter with poverty. Corrupt Indonesian police officers are solely interested in making money to enrich themselves, even if such outcomes occur at the expense of exploiting impoverished households in urban slums or rural areas. Corrupt police prefer to extort people unlawfully, accept bribes to turn a blind eye to criminal offences or acquire people's properties illegally (Buttle, Graham, and Meliala 2016). Such cultural deviance in the form of corruption deepens Indonesia's problem of poverty and economic inequalities. Many Indonesian nationals, especially those who are more excluded, isolated and deprived, are at high risk of struggling to secure any public services they are supposed to receive.

Police corruption, also, undermines the rule of law. Whenever corrupt police officers are in charge of the local authority, the application of the rule of law and justice is heavily skewed towards their interest (Buttle, Graham, and Meliala 2016). Therefore, the judiciary and legal system are substantially undermined. Whenever the rule of law is not applied impartially and consistently, the outcomes of injustice and lawless vulnerability occur, perpetuating the issues of poverty and predatory exploitation.

Police corruption worsens the degree of economic inequalities in Indonesia. Corrupt police officers often allow illegal operations of businesses so long as the business owners can afford to bribe their way through the opaque law enforcement and justice systems. The underprivileged cohorts who lack financial resources are, however, unable to secure sufficient monetary assets to bribe corrupt police officers. Such a circumstance results in the fact that more privileged Indonesian nationals can, through police corruption, take advantage of the institutional loopholes of Indonesia to secure more, both legal and especially illegal, economic opportunities. This means the wealth gap in Indonesia is widened, compounding the relative socio-economic disadvantages suffered by underprivileged populations.

Police corruption is one of the root causes that undermines governance, hampering Indonesia from realizing socio-economic development. Corrupt police practices, in many circumstances, often happen along with other government insufficiencies, such as the inadequacy of public service delivery, the ineffective allocation of public resources and the inability to curb organized (sex) crime. These institutional weaknesses help strengthen criminal actors' networks. More women and children are, therefore, concerningly vulnerable to facing any form of sexual exploitation.

There are multiple reasons why Indonesian police officers share the tendency to be corrupt. Aside from the established historical and cultural deviance, police corruption could happen due to the lack of proper supervision, low salary levels and the encounter with poverty (Quah 2022). Police officers facing these circumstances are more likely to resort to unethical practices, including extortion and bribery, to supplement their income. As a consequence, Indonesian police officers have gained a notorious reputation for being corrupt, compounding the levels of public distrust and lack of confidence in the law enforcement system.

Police officers are supposed to be involved in curbing prostitution and sex trafficking activities by arresting suspected sex criminal offenders. However, corrupt police officers, very often in Indonesian contexts, collude with paedophiles and sex traffickers to make financial gains through their engagement in prostitution and sex trafficking activities (Missbach 2015). When law enforcement authorities are simultaneously the criminal offenders (who receive little to no legal consequences), sexually exploited victims can hardly receive any form of justice. Corrupt police officers usually allow perpetrators to continue with their sexually illegal activities without any fear of assuming legal responsibilities. As a result, the entrenched issues of police corruption illustrate how weak the law enforcement system has been in Indonesia. Eradicating police corruption is one of the core parts of institutional reform that Indonesia has to undergo.

Unless the Indonesian government takes more stringent measures to eradicate the ingrained problem of corruption, underprivileged cohorts can hardly be effectively socio-economically empowered and protected and Indonesia's justice system can difficulty be refined. Addressing corruption within Indonesia's justice system is, hence, the core piece to attenuate the holistic package of socio-economic and institutional root causes of prostitution and sex trafficking. Only by building a corruption-free society can children be protected from facing any form of sexual exploitation and sex trafficking victimization.

INDONESIA'S POLICY GAPS IN STRENGTHENING ITS GOVERNANCE

Like the preceding chapter, here I am going to highlight the policy examination and recommendations to deconstruct the barriers to curbing prostitution and sex trafficking in Indonesia. In the following sections, I focus on institutional barriers to crackdowns on the sex industry. I delineate the policy gaps and recommendations for improving the institutional systems that hamper women and girls in Indonesia from being sexually exploited and engaging in prostitution. I identify the major policy gaps in strengthening the governance and law enforcement systems of the Indonesian government and address the country's police corruption issues, followed by providing policy recommendations accordingly to address such gaps per se.

A primary issue with Indonesia's governance is the lack of awareness in the Indonesian government about the magnitude and severity of sex work and trafficking. The Indonesian government has an absence of a proper, continuous data collection system, disallowing academic scholars and policy analysts to investigate the accurate number of women and children involved in sex work, alongside how these sexually exploited victims are distributed across the country. Indonesia is home to ample indigenous groups and many remote areas/islands. Given the ethnical and geographical structure, Indonesia can hardly collect primary data to obtain an estimate of the size of the sexually exploited population. The impotence of the Indonesian government to collect such data limits its design and implementation of effective policies to mitigate the problems of sex work (Nuraeny 2017).

The Indonesian government, furthermore, faces multiple shortcomings when forming its law enforcement. Indonesian police officers have been, at times, denounced for failing to arrest and prosecute sex traffickers and conventional sex establishment owners. Brothel owners, given the criminalization and religious unacceptance of commercial sex, often operate in secret areas and are well-protected by corrupt law enforcement officials, discouraging the non-corrupt police officers from applying effective raids to arrest whoever is involved in sexual transactions. Some local governing agencies, in addition, experience the problems of understaffed and under-resourced circumstances, in which law enforcement authorities lack proper professional training on handling and curbing prostitution and sex trafficking activities (Horgan and Braddock 2010). Given the weak governance, those facing little to no legal consequences for engaging in the delivery of commercial sex continue to sexually exploit children with impunity.

Indonesia experiences a shortage of financial resources to support anti-sex-trafficking activities. The inadequacy of resources makes the Indonesian government difficult to establish rehabilitation and education programmes for sex trafficking victims. Without these programmes, rescued sex trafficking victims are unable to receive the necessary healthcare support as well as the vocational skills that are favoured when integrating into society (Frazee 2015). To date, Indonesia does not have a specific budget distributed to the responsible local law enforcement units to curb commercial sex. As a result, Indonesia encounters limited capacity to empower underprivileged cohorts and combat commercial sex in an effective, efficient and consistent fashion (ibid.). More capacity-building endeavours have to be implemented to maximize the values of domestic law enforcement authorities in a way to curb prostitution and sex trafficking activities, ultimately, minimizing the rates of extramarital sex, including commercial sex, in Indonesia in the long run.

INDONESIA'S POLICY RECOMMENDATIONS ON STRENGTHENING ITS GOVERNANCE

In response to the policy gaps concerning Indonesia's governance, in this section, I present some policy recommendations that should be taken into account to strengthen the country's governing capacity. First, the Indonesian government has to strengthen its legal framework, enabling effective prosecution of whoever is involved in prostitution and sex trafficking. There is a need to tighten the existing law by introducing measures that help elaborate on female and child protection and offer more punitive sanctions to those found guilty of involvement in prostitution and sex trafficking. When more punitive terms are applied, Indonesia can deter potential perpetrators, as a cornerstone to enhance the safety levels of local communities for women and children.

The Indonesian government should also invest in the creation of awareness campaigns and education programmes for the general public, including underprivileged and vulnerable households and minors. Education is an essential instrument to prevent the practice of or involvement in prostitution and sex trafficking as such a cultural asset helps empower people with knowledge about the risks and rights each person should be given. More professional training schemes should be offered and made compulsory for local police and welfare officers, especially in rural areas where the quality of the authorities is in question, in order to facilitate their recognition and management of exploitation cases promptly and aptly. Education campaigns in educational (such as schools and universities) and public (such as public services centres) institutions should convey messages that educate about the dangers involved in sex work, helping deter underprivileged cohorts from being lured into the sex trade and empower the general public to combat the existing social stigmatization of prostitution and sex trafficking.

The Indonesian government should, moreover, tighten its welfare systems to provide sufficient support to sexual victims of prostitution and sex trafficking. More social workers, psychologists and medical experts should be made available in regions, including villages, that are identified and recognized as the supply hub of sex workers or sex tourist-popular destinations. The Indonesian government should engage with NGOs who have experience in the field of empowering underprivileged cohorts from being sexually exploited and collaboratively develop programmes for victim support, rehabilitation and reintegration into society. The delivery of support and care for the sex crime victims helps ease the trauma they have encountered and enables them to comply with morality and religious, social and cultural norms.

Raising the levels of resource allocation that allow Indonesian nationals to report cases of sex work and trafficking should be prioritized. The Indonesian government should invest in technology to enhance the identification of sex crime offenders, allow trafficking of their movements, and monitor the activities of sex trades. More funding and training programmes should be distributed to upskill police officers and judicial authorities, enabling these professionals to collaborate with international law enforcement agencies for intellectual exchange and cracking down on transnational sex crime groups. These policy focuses are essential to helping Indonesia strengthen its governing capacity that, in turn, facilitates the country to curb sex work.

INDONESIA'S POLICY GAPS IN STRENGTHENING ITS LAW ENFORCEMENT SYSTEM

Alongside Indonesia's governance, the domestic law enforcement system has to be strengthened in order to combat any form of activities of commercial sex. A major policy gap concerning the weak law enforcement system is the shortage of coordination and communications between law enforcement agencies. Despite the presence of anti-human trafficking directorates and anti-trafficking task forces, Indonesia has an inadequacy of collaboration between these agencies (Subono and Kosandi 2019). The insufficient communication between agencies undermines law enforcement efforts and creates significant challenges in identifying and prosecuting perpetrators, resulting in low rates of sex crime convictions.

The Indonesian government is also facing a financial shortage concerning addressing sex crime issues. The implementation and evaluation of policies to address sex work and trafficking require substantial amounts of financial, technological and human resources. However, the Indonesian government is facing limited financial capacity which results in difficulties in arranging and applying effective measures to curb these illegal activities.

Furthermore, Indonesia's legal system lacks legislation that specifically addresses sex work and trafficking. Despite the country's Penal Code and Indonesian Penal Procedure Code criminalizing human trafficking, Indonesia fails to have any specific provision to address child sex trafficking for commercial sexual exploitation purposes (Isnawati 2021). The existing policy gaps weaken law enforcement efforts, discouraging the identification and prosecution of perpetrators.

Moreover, there is a shortage of accountability for law enforcement officers within Indonesia. Such a circumstance can be demonstrated by the severity of police and judicial corruption that undermines sex crime investigations and prosecutions. The shortage of sufficient resources, coupled with the lack of accountability, contributes to the dissatisfactory rate of sex crime convictions, perpetuating the problems of prostitution and sex trafficking.

Moreover, the Indonesian government has very limited outreach and prevention programmes to address the root causes (Whitford et al. 2021), as identified in Chapters 3 and 4, of prostitution and sex trafficking. There is a lack of awareness and education on topics in relation to such sex crimes. With the lack of relevant awareness and knowledge, the effectiveness and scales of law enforcement efforts to curb prostitution and sex trafficking are lacking and limited, in which the root causes per se are not sufficiently addressed.

To conclude, the Indonesian government has limited coordination and collaboration efforts between law enforcement agencies. Also, the local governing agencies are often underfunded and understaffed, coupled with the limited accountability held by law enforcement officers. With these policy gaps, alongside the weak, ineffective and inconsistent legislation efforts, the Indonesian government has, to date, failed to create a sustainable and apt approach to curb sex work and trafficking domestically.

INDONESIA'S POLICY RECOMMENDATIONS ON STRENGTHENING ITS LAW ENFORCEMENT SYSTEM

To strengthen Indonesia's law enforcement system, a primary policy recommendation is the need to strengthen the enforcement of existing regulations and laws. Owing to the weak law enforcement system and corruption culture, Indonesia's laws against the practice of sex work and trafficking are not adequately and consistently enforced, resulting in rampant violations. Here the Indonesian government has to form a robust legal framework, provide sufficient training, education and awareness-building programmes for law enforcers, and develop more legal and non-legal supportive policies that help empower the prosecution and conviction of sex crime offenders.

It is important to raise awareness of the dangers, risks and costs of involvement in prostitution and sex trafficking. As addressed, many victims of the sex industry come from impoverished, deprived and distanced origins, and may have limited to no awareness of the risks associated with prostitution and sex trafficking activities. The Indonesian government and domestic civic and religious organizations have to make concerted efforts to educate households and local communities on the dangers, risks and costs associated with sex work. Building stronger public awareness can aid the identification and reporting of sex crimes.

Simultaneously, the Indonesian government has to raise the accountability of whoever is involved in prostitution and sex trafficking. Not only do I refer to the sex traffickers, pimps and conventional sex establishment owners, but also the law enforcement officials who collude with the sex criminal offenders. With stronger, stricter and more punitive regulations and law enforcement procedures, perpetrators of sex work and trafficking acts can be brought to justice in order to attenuate the prevalence of such sex crime incidences. As a result, so long as the Indonesian government can build a more organized and better-structured law enforcement system, the Government can create a safer environment for its citizens, including women and children who are of underprivileged status.

INDONESIA'S POLICY GAPS IN ADDRESSING POLICE CORRUPTION

Despite the acknowledgement of the severity of police corruption, the Indonesian government is subject to significant policy gaps that hamper its progress in addressing prostitution and sex trafficking. A primary policy gap in Indonesia is the shortage of comprehensive and effective monitoring mechanisms that are designed to identify police corruption cases in relation to prostitution and sex trafficking. Indonesia's development of a regulatory framework for tackling the problem of police corruption is held responsible by multiple governing units. With the limited inter-agency communications and coordination, the Indonesian government experiences substantial difficulties in identifying and addressing the issues of police corruption. Perpetrators are, as a result, free from facing any legal consequences, a circumstance that leaves underprivileged, vulnerable women and children to be continually sexually exploited.

Indonesia is, moreover, subject to the inadequacy of resources and initiatives distribution that help address the root causes of sex work and trafficking. Despite Indonesia having multiple laws and regulations that are designed to combat prostitution and sex trafficking, such legal efforts are often undermined by the governmental underfunded situations. Furthermore, due to the limited financial capacity, there are inadequate programmes or support systems to offer vulnerable women and children alternative paths to sex work. These alternatives include reintegration into the education and labour market. With the shortage of these alternatives, more underprivileged women prefer staying in the sex industry as a means to secure subsistence and financial resources. Addressing these policy gaps requires a comprehensive and coordinated approach that involves all relevant stakeholders to address the root causes of prostitution and create apt measures for monitoring, preventing and sanctioning police corruption effectively. The Indonesian government has to ensure that the locally responsible governing agencies are financially sufficient to arrange and deliver legal, institutional and social intervention packages that holistically help underprivileged women and children to be rescued from being sexually exploited. Only by curbing police corruption can these governing agencies enjoy adequate financial capacities—because corrupt police and law enforcement authorities at large often exploit the loose justice system and unlawfully take away parts of the public resources that are supposed to be allocated for social protection and pro-poor development purposes.

Indonesia's Policy Recommendations on Addressing Police Corruption

In order to curb the issues of ingrained police corruption, I present some policy recommendations that have to be taken into consideration. First, Indonesia has to build a stronger political will to tackle the problems of corruption (Manullang 2020). Increasing law enforcement authorities' salary levels and welfare packages and enforcing stricter disciplinary measures for those who participate in corrupt activities are policy goals that are conducive to reducing the rates of police corruption. The application of stricter disciplinary measures to tackle police corruption can only be effectively delivered should top-ranked law enforcement authorities themselves lead by example to denounce and reject any corrupt practices. These top-ranked authorities include police and local governing bureau chiefs.

Also, more education and awareness-building programmes in relation to sex work and trafficking have to be held. Here police officers have to be trained to learn how to properly identify and investigate organized sex crimes, in addition to informing the general public about the dangers, costs, risks and consequences of participation in sex work and trafficking activities. The Indonesian government has to closely collaborate with community-based organizations to deliver community outreach programmes and support services that help identify vulnerable women and children working in the sex industry, as well as help rescue them from continually facing sexual exploitation of any form.

More collaboration and information sharing between all involved agencies and jurisdictions have to be arranged and practised, especially when organized sex crime is often transnational in nature. Indonesia can, from a broader understanding, establish partnerships and agreements with neighbouring countries to share cost-effective practices for curbing prostitution and sex trafficking. Indonesia should, in addition, actively co-work with international organizations including the United Nations, the Asian Development Bank, the World Bank and the Association of Southeast Asian Nations (ASEAN) to further enhance the circulation of expertise, advice and information concerning the development of legal and regulatory frameworks to curb sex work and trafficking.

CONCLUSION

Indonesia needs to strengthen its political will, law enforcement and justice systems and socio-legal framework to enhance the institutional efficiency in curbing commercial sex. When Indonesia criminalizes extramarital sex and aims at complying with Islamic law to prohibit any form of sexual intimacy beyond marital relationships, the Indonesian government must address its institutional loopholes that allow Indonesian nationals, especially the male cohorts, to seek extramarital, casual sexual pleasure commercially. Optimizing the governance, the law enforcement system and the problem of ingrained corruption involved is necessary for Indonesia to build a more well-designed and -facilitated socio-legal structure that enables the law enforcement authorities to curb commercial sex and rescue whoever is being sexually exploited. Addressing the socio-economic and institutional root causes of prostitution and sex trafficking should be implemented simultaneously. Without such a holistic approach, the presence of socio-economic root causes of prostitution would facilitate the existence of institutional counterparts, and vice versa.

References

Antara News. 2022. "Indonesia Ranks 130th on Human Development Index: BKKBN". 7 December 2022. https://en.antaranews.com/news/264243/indonesia-ranks-130th-on-human-development-index-bkkbn#:~:text="Data%20from%20the%20 World%20Bank,Forum"%20in%20Jakarta%20on%20Tuesday (accessed 9 March 2023).

Arifin, T., I. Trinugroho, M. Prabowo, S. Sutaryo, and M. Muhtar. 2015. "Local Governance and Corruption: Evidence from Indonesia". *Corporate Ownership and Control* 12, no. 4: 194–99.

Awaludin, A. 2019. "The Uncertainty of Regulating Online Prostitution in Indonesia". *Proceedings of the 3rd International Conference on Globalisation of Law and Local Wisdom* (ICGLOW 2019). https://doi.org/10.2991/icglow-19.2019.81

Buttle, J., S. Graham, and A. Meliala. 2016. "A Cultural Constraints Theory of Police Corruption: Understanding the Persistence of Police Corruption in Contemporary Indonesia". *Australian & New Zealand Journal of Criminology* 49, no. 3: 437–54.

Davies, S., L. Stone, and J. Buttle. 2016. "Covering Cops: Critical Reporting of Indonesian Police Corruption". *Pacific Journalism Review* 22, no. 2: 185–201.

Dick, H., and J. Mulholland. 2016. "The Politics of Corruption in Indonesia". Georgetown *Journal of International Affairs* 17, no. 1: 43–49.

Frazee, S. 2015. "Assessing the Impact of CSR Policy and Practice of Education of Orphans and Vulnerable Children in Indonesia". *International Commerce and Policy Theses*. https://scholar.valpo.edu/icp_mstheses/1 (accessed 26 March 2023).

Horgan, J., and K. Braddock. 2010. "Rehabilitating the Terrorists? Challenges in Assessing the Effectiveness of De-Radicalisation Programmes". *Terrorism and Political Violence* 22, no. 2: 267–91.

Isnawati, M. 2021. "The Urgence of Indonesian Penal Code (KUHP) Reform to Realise Humanistic-Based Imprisonment". *Borobudur Law Review* 3, no. 1: 78–83.

Jauhari, I. 2014. "A Comparison of Child Protection Law between Indonesia and Malaysia". *Indonesian Journal of International Law* 12, no. 1: Article 5. https://scholarhub.ui.ac.id/ijil/vol12/iss1/5

Missbach, A. 2015. "Making a 'Career' in People-Smuggling in Indonesia: Protracted Transit, Restricted Mobility and the Lack of Legal Work Rights". *Sojourn: Journal of Social Issues in Southeast Asia* 30, no. 2: 423–54.

Manullang, S. 2020. "The Online Prostitution Act from Legal Sociology Perspective in Indonesia". *International Research Journal of Management, IT and Social Sciences* 7, no. 4: 36–42.

Nuraeny, H. 2017. "Trafficking of Migrant Workers in Indonesia: A Legal Enforcement and Economic Perspective of Prevention and Protection Efforts". *European Research Studies Journal* 20, no. 4B: 16–26.

Quah, J. 2022. "Combating Police Corruption in Five Asian Countries: A Comparative Analysis". *Asian Education and Development Studies* 9, no. 2: 197–216.

Ramli, M. 2022. "Hasil Survei: Polisi Indonesia Tempati Peringkat Pertama Paling Korup di Asia Tenggara" [Survey Results: Indonesian Police Rank First Most Corrupt in Southeast Asia]. *Berita Baru*. https://beritabaru.co/hasil-survei-polisi-indonesia-tempati-peringkat-pertama-paling-korup-di-asia-tenggara/

Riswanda, R. 2015. "Public Education and Capacity Building to Address the Rights of Marginalised through Critical Reflection on Prostitution Discourses in Indonesia". *Participatory Educational Research* 2, no. 4: 74–100.

———, Y. Nantes, and J. Mills. 2016. "Re-Framing Prostitution in Indonesia: A Critical Systemic Approach". *Systemic Practice and Action Research* 29: 517–39. https://doi.org/10.1007/s11213-016-9379-2

Sofyani, H., S. Pratolo, and Z. Saleh. 2022. "Do Accountability and Transparency Promote Community Trust? Evidence from Village Government in Indonesia". *Journal of Accounting and Organisational Change* 18, no. 3: 397–418.

Subono, N., and M. Kosandi. 2019. "The Regionalism Paradox in the Fight against Human Trafficking: Indonesia and the Limits of Regional Cooperation in ASEAN". *Journal of Leadership, Accountability and Ethics* 16, no. 2: 89–98.

Transparency International. 2023. "Corruption Perceptions Index". https://www.transparency.org/en/cpi/2022/index/idn

Whitford, K., E. Mitchell, E. Lazuardi, E. Rowe, I. Tasya, D. Wirawan, R. Wisaksana, Y. Subronto, H. Prameswari, J. Kaldor, and S. Bell. 2021. "Corrigendum to: A Strengths-Based Analysis of Social Influences that Enhance HIV Testing among Female Sex Workers in Urban Indonesia". *Sexual Health* 18, no. 1: 122.

5

Visiting Indonesia's Anti-Extramarital Sex Legislation

ABSTRACT

This chapter visits the latest legislation on passing the criminal code of criminalizing people who practise extramarital sex in Indonesia. I argue how criminalization alone, without relevant socio-economic empowerment and well-organized institutional mechanisms presented in Chapters 3 and 4 respectively, cannot crack down on the sex industry. Supported by the relevant scholarly discourse presented in this book thus far, I believe that commercial sex activities should remain rampant, to some degree, in the domestic underground economy, or more local prostitutes should be trafficked to neighbouring sex tourism hubs, including Bangkok, Pattaya, Phnom Penh and Manila, to work as migrant sex workers. I stress the importance of both local and regional collaboration to tighten intra- and international anti-prostitution policies to curtail the supply of sex workers within Indonesia and Southeast Asia at large.

INTRODUCTION

This chapter visits Indonesia's latest criminalization against extramarital sex, including commercial sex. I discuss how contextually important it is for Indonesia, as the largest Muslim-majority country in the world, to discourage, if not eliminate, extramarital sex, both commercially and non-commercially. I, then, engage in the scholarly discourse on how the country cannot crack down on its extramarital sex without eradicating the socio-economic and institutional root causes of commercial sex. In

Southeast Asia, sex tourism, prostitution and sex trafficking are rampant and normalized to some degree (Curley 2014; Dahles 2009). Eradicating these root causes is the ultimate solution to Indonesia's decision to punitively bar local populations from engaging in extramarital sex. Both intranational and international policies will be highlighted and summarized in this chapter to present how Indonesia can address the issues of sex work and trafficking at its best in the long term.

CONTEXTUAL IMPORTANCE OF CRACKDOWN ON EXTRAMARITAL SEX IN INDONESIA

In Indonesia, per Islamic law, extramarital sex has been religiously and politically seen as immoral, wrongful and socially undesirable (Crouch 2009). Premarital sex, extramarital sex, queer sex and commercial sex have all been labelled as immoral sex in Indonesian society. Owing to gendered freedom restriction and cultural norms, there is a general expectation throughout Indonesia that men will have extramarital sex, as per *Sex and Sexualities in Contemporary Indonesia: Sexual Politics, Health, Diversity and Representations* (Bennett and Davies 2015). Despite the prevalence, extramarital affairs, especially those committed by female cohorts, are highly condemned in Indonesian society. As already mentioned in this book, extramarital affairs, in Indonesia, are not a new phenomenon. Nevertheless, in recent years, Indonesia's parliament has been discussing the possibility of criminalizing extramarital sex. While banning any form of extramaritally sexual activities is controversial as dissidents denounce such a legislative intervention as against the interests of personal freedom, however, given the historical and cultural support of the practice of Islamic law, Indonesia's parliament passed the criminal code on criminalizing extramarital sex on 6 December 2022 (Black and Jung 2014; Teresia and Lamb 2022). In recent years when policymakers had been discussing whether an anti-extramarital sex law should be passed, dissidents had made a valuable point that addressing more pressing issues like poverty, economic inequalities, corruption and institutional loopholes should be prioritized (Davies 2014; Dewi and Dartanto 2019). The preceding chapters delineated how important it is for Indonesia to address these socio-economically and institutionally contributing factors of commercial sex and poor governance in Indonesian contexts. There is a sequence to build a more sustainable future in Indonesia. Empowering women and children socio-economically and reforming the institutional mechanisms systematically help lower the prevalence of sex work. With a shrinking supply of prostitution, the markets for the sex trade and sex tourism will curtail gradually. Law enforcement authorities and policymakers can narrow their focus on applying intervention policies to curb prostitution when the size of the sex industry curtails. Fewer underprivileged Indonesian cohorts will be subject to physical and sexual exploitation and abuse, but will become a socially-contributing labour force. Indonesia becomes more liveable with a decreased level of prostitution-related crime rates. More domestic and foreign investments and business development, in the long term, will be seen within the country so long as Indonesia can present itself as a socially cohesive and stable society and economy. As a result, the growth of Indonesian populations will be socio-economically empowered and disincentivized from entering the sex industry.

In the following, I will detail how eliminating the pressing issues of the root causes of prostitution is of utmost importance while criminalizing extramarital sex is secondary. Regardless of whether extramarital sex is criminalized, extramarital affairs, such as engagement in paid sex, will continue to occur in Indonesia so long as the root causes of commercial sex are not eradicated.

In Indonesian contexts, extramarital sex is more than simply a moral violation but also a legal issue. By criminalizing extramarital sex, Indonesia's parliament delivers a strong message that extramarital affairs, regardless of their prevalence, would not be tolerated to a large extent in the hope of discouraging Indonesian nationals from violating such a law (Setiawan 2022). Moral values aside, extramarital sex criminalization does, in fact, help generate some forms of pragmatic benefits to Indonesian society and the local population. For example, criminalizing extramarital sex helps discourage the infection and circulation of sexually transmitted diseases. The introductory chapter argued how common it is for Indonesian sex workers to contract sexually transmitted diseases and how irregular and inconsistent they had been practising safe commercial sex (Winarto et al. 2023). Criminalizing extramarital sex, which indirectly legally discourages Indonesian nationals from engaging in commercial sex, would help deter the spread of domestic HIV/AIDS and other sexually transmitted diseases (Arimbi, Putra, and Hapsari 2022).

Extramarital sex criminalization is also an intervention that helps prevent women from being physically abused. Husbands have the disposition to apply violence against their wives if the latter is caught cheating and having extramarital affairs (Mas'udah 2020). By cracking down on extramarital sex from a legal standpoint, Indonesia's parliament is endeavouring to discourage married couples from having extramarital affairs, that, indirectly, lowers the incidences of marital conflicts and violence. By cracking down on extramarital sex, Indonesia's parliament is, additionally, demonstrating its commitment to complying with Islamic values and principles (Supardin and Syatar 2021). Such conformity is deemed necessary to maintain social and religious cohesion and harmony respectively in Indonesian contexts.

Building a lower tolerance of extramarital sex is, therefore, generating benefits beyond the satisfaction of Islamic moral values. Such a governmental attitude helps pragmatically reduce the costs and risks certain disadvantaged populations are exposed to, in order to help promote a more organized and secure society.

Contextual Importance of Crackdown on Commercial Sex in Indonesia

In the preceding chapters, this book focused on the discussion of the construction of commercial sex and how engagement in prostitution poses a variety of costs and risks to Indonesian vulnerable populations and society as a whole. Here commercial sex has been closely linked to human trafficking, an international menace which breaches human rights and exploits the most underprivileged cohorts. Women and children are particularly affected by the rampant commercial sex and sex trafficking activities. Cracking down on extramarital sex, including commercial sex, is an essential step towards the elimination of human trafficking, and any underlying human rights violations, in Indonesia.

Commercial sex is, moreover, closely linked to the abuse of drugs and other psychoactive substances. This is because sex workers working in conventional sex and entertainment establishments are given constant exposure to the opportunities to gain access to these entertainment substances (Jainah et al. 2022). So long as the prevalence of commercial sex is attenuated, the market for drug trade and drug purchase would curtail, minimizing the public health and social costs Indonesia has to bear which are imposed by the incidences of drug abuse.

In Indonesia, despite normalization to some degree, sex beyond marriage is often deemed taboo (Shibuya et al. 2023). While Indonesia, like neighbouring Southeast Asian countries such as Thailand, has been pressured to legalize commercial sex work as a means to protect the safety, health and well-being of legal sex workers (Charoensuthipan 2023), local Indonesian customs and traditions demonstrate that prostitution breaches the national values that Muslim-majority Indonesia follows. Cracking down on prostitution will help reaffirm Indonesia's cultural, traditional and national values whilst promoting the implementation of relevant law enforcement endeavours. Therefore, cracking down on commercial sex, as much as eliminating extramarital sex, is contextually important and valuable in Indonesia, regardless of the feasibility concerns.

COMMERCIAL SEX AND EXTRAMARITAL SEX

As a Muslim-majority country, Islamic teachings and practices shape Indonesian society's cultural norms, identities and values. In some conservative Islamic communities in Indonesia, it is noteworthy that those who are caught performing extramarital sex could be punished to death (Muhyidin, Adhi, and Triyono 2022). In Indonesian and Islamic contexts, the criminalization of extramarital sex is deemed an essential step for the country to uphold religious and moral identities and values to a large degree.

Despite the sins of having extramarital affairs, commercial sex has been a long-standing issue in Indonesia. Despite the illegal nature, prostitution has been prevalent in major tourist-popular Indonesian regions, including Bali and the city of Jakarta (Hulsbergen and Nooteboom 2022). Both domestic and international sex tourists visit local conventional sex and entertainment establishments to seek commercial sex, indirectly allowing the growth of organized sex crimes, such as human trafficking, within the country (ibid.). With the prevalence of sex crimes, the Indonesian government has faced substantial difficulties in cracking down on extramarital sex given how often this is closely intertwined with commercial sex. To criminalize extramarital sex, the Indonesian government has, therefore, to take a more aggressive stance towards eradicating the root causes of commercial sex to facilitate the regulation of any sanction against extramarital sex.

Cracking down on commercial sex is, hence, contextually necessary for Indonesia to foster its criminalization of extramarital sex for the benefit of preserving domestic cultural values, social harmony and religious norms. The Indonesian government must tighten its regulation of the sex industry and provide more welfare support and social protection for vulnerable prostitutes as vital steps to build a more just, equitable and liveable society that fulfils morality and respect for the sanctity of marital relationships in the long run (Saputraa and Emovwodo 2022).

SOCIO-ECONOMIC ROOT CAUSES OF COMMERCIAL SEX AND EXTRAMARITAL SEX

Criminalizing extramarital sex may seem like a logical response to preserve Islamic values. However, extramarital affairs cannot be prohibited unless the criminalization is accompanied by endeavours to address the underlying socio-economic root causes of sex work. Poverty and inequality are the core problems causing the prevalence of prostitution and sex trafficking (Ridho and Siswantoro 2023). Women and girls, especially those who are marginalized, discriminated against and deprived are propelled to enter the sex industry owing to their constant encounters with denial to seek opportunities for economic advancement (Munro 2023). Without incorporating law enforcement measures to enhance the favourability of these women and children in the education and labour markets, more of them will continue to enter the sex industry. With a sufficient supply of sex workers, the prevalence of prostitution can hardly be alleviated in Indonesia, leading to the challenges of prevailing extramarital affairs.

Criminalizing extramarital sex alone is ineffective in curbing extramarital affairs. Criminalization may even exacerbate the problems of sex work and trafficking as more women and children are pushed into the underground economy which makes relevant law enforcement endeavours and humanitarian aid delivery more impotent (Fuadi et al. 2022). Women and children who are sexually, physically and even financially exploited would face further discrimination, abuse and vulnerability as the underground sex networks are hard to monitor and regulate (Bah 2022).

Banning extramarital sex may ostensibly seem like a direct solution to address the issue of prostitution and sex trafficking in Indonesia. However, criminalizing extramarital sex alone fails to address the complex socio-economic issues that impose the consolidation of the societal problem of the prevalence of sex work. Therefore, the preceding chapters primarily focused on discussing how policies should be shaped to alleviate, or even eradicate, the socio-economic root causes of prostitution and sex trafficking. By empowering women and children socio-economically, they become less vulnerable to facing sexual exploitation that, in turn, curtails the prevalence of the sex industry and extramarital affairs.

INSTITUTIONAL ROOT CAUSES OF COMMERCIAL SEX AND EXTRAMARITAL SEX

Like the importance of eradicating the socio-economic root causes of sex work, Indonesian policymakers have to actively address the institutional root causes in order to crack down on the domestic sex industry and curb any sex trafficking activities. Without eliminating the institutional root causes of prostitution and sex trafficking, the Indonesian government cannot feasibly tackle the problems of commercial sex and, from a broader perspective, extramarital sex.

As mentioned in the preceding chapter, the Indonesian government lacks an effective regulation system and control plan to curtail the prevalence of sex work (Martha, Setiabudhi, and Setyorini 2022). Sex trafficking and prostitution continue to persist in many parts of Indonesia, especially in areas that are popular for tourists, including sex tourists. Without addressing the institutional root causes of sex work and trafficking, underprivileged cohorts would continue to rely on the sex industry as a channel to satisfy their survival needs. Especially in tourist-popular regions where cultural acceptance of commercial sex happens to some degree, underprivileged cohorts, despite being illegal and immoral in nature, may enter the sex industry owing to their entitlement to limited alternative, legitimate choices to seek economic opportunities (Pangestu, Yuhastina, and Rahman 2022). With more women and children entering the sex industry, however, the gender-biased cultural deviance that deems females as commodifiable and subordinate would heighten, leading to more long-term discrimination and stigmatization against female cohorts within and beyond the sex industry. With a deteriorating problem of gender inequality, Indonesia will face more obstacles to eradicating sexual exploitation against women and girls in the long run.

In Indonesia, the Indonesian government has to build a stronger, better-regulated mechanism that is conducive to the promotion of public trust towards the government. Also, with the application of relevant policies to tighten its institutional mechanism, the Indonesian police force, in theory, should be on the pathway to becoming a less corrupt body. Corruption is a significant form of cultural deviance within institutional settings. Tackling corruption and improving the levels of public confidence towards the police force help minimize the Indonesian public's fear of crime and the application of a higher degree of formal and informal social control can be facilitated.

In conclusion, without addressing the institutional root causes of prostitution and sex trafficking, banning extramarital sex in Indonesia is an ineffective solution. To truly tackle these problems, the government must focus on holistically providing more resources to strengthen the capacity of local governing agencies that are responsible for curbing prostitution and sex trafficking activities. When institutional loopholes that favour the prevalence of sex work are addressed properly, organized crime groups would no longer deem Indonesia a haven for the arrangement and operation of illegal businesses. Such a societal outcome, in turn, is conducive to the realization of Indonesia's goal of attenuating commercial sex and extramarital sex.

WHAT ELSE IS NEEDED TO CRACK DOWN ON EXTRAMARITAL SEX

I reiterate that Indonesia is unlikely to be able to ban extramarital sex without cracking down on commercial sex. Within the country, commercial sex, despite being significantly culturally stigmatized, provides a source of temptation and opportunity for Indonesian nationals to seek extramarital affairs. Indonesia's recent efforts to heighten the anti-prostitution law enforcement have been conducive to the country's promotion of criminalizing extramarital sex. In 2019, for example, the Indonesian government launched a new wave of campaigns to curb sex work and trafficking in Indonesia. Here the Indonesian government tightened law enforcement efforts to crack down on commercial sex activities and set up hotlines for sexually exploited victims to report cases of abuse (Simorangkir and Schumacher 2022). While such endeavours are commendable, they are insufficient to effectively prohibit extramarital sex unless holistic, comprehensive packages of policies and interventions, discussed in the previous two chapters, are consistently and tightly exercised to crack down on the sex industry correspondingly. People who are tempted to engage in extramarital affairs may prefer to seek psychological, emotional and sexual excitement and/or satisfaction, as they may find the marital relationship boring and unfulfilling. The availability of commercial sex engagement may, therefore, be seen as an easily accessible means to seek such excitation and/or satisfaction.

Banning commercial sex may be an admirable goal to help minimize any affairs beyond marital relationships. However, the prohibition of commercial sex is insufficient to help eradicate the prevalence of extramarital sex in Indonesia. To effectively attenuate the prevalence of extramarital affairs, the Indonesian government has to address the underlying psychological and emotional unfulfillment that contributes to such a deviant, immoral practice. For example, community-based organizations including religious institutions should actively promote the psychological and emotional fulfilment that can be earned by following the norms of fidelity and respecting traditional, conventional values.

EXTRAMARITAL SEX CRIMINALIZATION AND THE PREVALENCE OF COMMERCIAL SEX IN THE UNDERGROUND ECONOMY

Having a thriving underground sex economy is nothing new to Southeast Asia, including Indonesia. Such an underground sex economy in Indonesia operates outside of legal regulation. Here businesses specializing in the provision of sexual transactions and human trafficking for sexual purposes can often be found (Ridho and Nurhayati 2022). When extramarital sex has been criminalized, more Indonesian nationals and prostitutes are expected to seek sexual transaction opportunities in more hidden, covert settings. Both the rights and security of commercial sex clients and providers are not protected in these settings.

Sex traffickers and conventional sex establishment owners are expected to offer commercial sex services to those who are unable to access them lawfully. Usually, a premium price is charged when services are provided unlawfully, which, in turn, leads to more profitability enjoyed by criminal syndicates. These syndicates may look for opportunities to expand their businesses in the underground economy so long as they are profitable (Hamid 2022).

With the shortage of government regulation of the underground sex industry, more unregulated—such as unsafe—commercial sex is expected to be performed. The lack of regulation renders the heightened risks of spreading sexually transmitted diseases. As a result, Indonesia is subject to heavier healthcare burdens and diminished productivity. The anti-extramarital sex policy of the Indonesian government could, therefore, result in unintended damage to both Indonesian populations and society. Criminalizing extramarital sex may counter-promote the engagement in commercial sex in underground, unregulated settings, providing more economic opportunities for sex traffickers to expand the scale of their unlawful businesses. Therefore, when extramarital sex has been criminalized to satisfy the moral and religious expectations outlined in Islamic laws, the Indonesian government has to concentrate on delivering interventions to empower socio-economically disadvantaged cohorts and strengthen its socio-legal frameworks and governing mechanisms that are conducive to the development of a more organized, prostitution-free society.

Extramarital Sex Criminalization and the Prevalence of Overseas Sex Work

When extramarital sex is criminalized and criminals can now be imprisoned for up to six months, more prostitutes or underprivileged cohorts on the verge of entering the sex industry may now relocate to other countries, especially to neighbouring Southeast Asian countries that house large sex tourism markets, to work as overseas or migrant sex workers (Mao 2022). Countries such as Thailand, Hong Kong and Singapore have a history of attracting migrant prostitutes from Indonesia (Hwang 2022). The commercial sex markets in these host countries are unlikely to diminish anytime soon. Especially when migrant sex workers have sexual networks in overseas host countries, they are prone to relocate to seek commercial sex-related economic opportunities.

Working as a migrant sex worker is, however, a vulnerable occupation. Women and underage cohorts choosing to work as migrant sex workers are exposed to higher risks of facing physical, sexual and financial harassment, exploitation and abuse, owing to their unfamiliarity with the domestic regulation policies (Hwang 2022). They may be, when needed, encountering more hurdles to accessing healthcare services and are at higher risk of contracting sexually transmitted diseases, including HIV/AIDS. Given the constant exploitation, abuse and harassment and the lack of social and public services support, these migrant sex workers could be vulnerable to the development of mental health issues which jeopardize their long-term health and well-being.

The Indonesian government has to take steps to address the root causes of prostitution, including the problems of poverty, the lack of education opportunities and the shortage of accessible public services. More remedies, including the policy recommendations discussed in the preceding two chapters, should be arranged and delivered to Indonesian prostitutes to allow them to be more empowered, to be given more life chances and to be entitled to more negotiating power if they end up working in the sex industry.

Intranational Policies to Curb Sex Work

Indonesia has to strengthen its domestic legal framework and law enforcement mechanisms to eradicate the root causes of commercial sex. Here sex trafficking and exploitation should be a prioritized agenda that Indonesian lawmakers and law enforcement authorities have to tackle. Law enforcement agencies have to be provided with needed cultural, professional and intellectual resources and training opportunities to improve their anti-prostitution work efficiency. Better trained, resourced and supported law enforcement officers, hence, have a higher capacity to arrest and prosecute sex crime violators severely punitively.

Indonesia has to raise public awareness by organizing freely accessible educational workshops or programmes to inform the drivers of and consequences of engaging in commercial sex. Such programmes should particularly be initiated and run in tourist-popular areas, such as Bali and the city of Jakarta, as more sex tourists are housed. The Indonesian government has to partner with state-run media channels (including mass media and social media platforms) to disseminate public education information that details how sex work is initiated and why sex workers are victims who deserve respect and support. Ultimately, the Indonesian government has to educate the general public about how Indonesia can be collectively built as a more socially inclusive community where, despite the presence of Islamic laws and the moral sins attached to prostitution, underprivileged cohorts being forced to enter the sex industry should be sympathized and helped.

There are ample domestic interventions that local policymakers can implement in order to raise the availability and accessibility of life chances among underprivileged women and children. Also, the underprivileged cohorts should constantly be positively socialized in domestic, school and organizational settings, allowing them to be socially controlled from expressing any form of criminality and delinquency. When they are positively socialized, they are also given opportunities to be healthily socially influenced which prompts their compliance with morality, social norms and religious obligations.

INTERNATIONAL POLICIES TO CURB SEX WORK

In addition to intranational endeavours, Indonesia should engage in international cooperation that facilitates its progress of curbing commercial sex. Indonesia has to strengthen partnerships with other, especially neighbouring, countries and organizations (such as the United Nations Convention Against Transnational Organized Crime) at both regional and global levels to address the root causes of paid sex effectively and consistently. Here Indonesia should focus on exchanging information, strategies, technologies and even human resources in order to enhance the domestic capacity building that is beneficial to eradicating prostitution (Novianti and Damayanti 2022).

Indonesia has to actively participate in the implementation of the United Nations Sustainable Development Goals (SDGs) that focus on championing gender equality, empowering women and children, and supporting sustained economic growth and favourable and safe working environments. The prostitution industry is major structural damage to females' access to empowerment and economic opportunities. Addressing SDGs on curbing gender inequalities and, therefore, commercial sex activities are needed in Indonesia (United Nations N.d.a; United Nations N.d.b).

Indonesia should, simultaneously, actively participate in the ASEAN Plan of Action against Trafficking in Persons, Especially Women and Children (2016–25). Here ASEAN members aim to collectively eliminate human trafficking within Southeast Asia by exchanging advice and intellectual resources and engaging in the discourse on anti-human trafficking policy evaluations (Franco 2023). By actively participating in the ASEAN Plan can Indonesia create a better-designed and more comprehensive regional response to the prevalence of prostitution.

Indonesia should endeavour to ramp up its efforts to combat commercial sex activities. Here the country has to participate in multi-dimensional complexities involved in the crackdowns on the sex industry. With more effective implementation of national, regional and international protocols and collaboration with other countries, Indonesia will be trending in the right direction concerning mitigating the issues of prevailing commercial sex and, at large, extramarital sex. As a result, Indonesia can build a safer and more secure society in a sustainable manner.

INDONESIA'S 2024 ELECTIONS

The National Commission on Human Rights (*Komnas HAM*) has announced its commitment to make 2024 Indonesia's presidential, parliamentary and regional elections a human rights-friendly event to ensure that all citizens, including those belonging to the marginalized and vulnerable groups, are included by local and national policymaking. Here *Komnas HAM* endeavours to make sure that all marginalized and vulnerable cohorts can access the elections and promotes the importance for all political parties to guarantee the consolidation of the values of freedom and fairness and respect human rights principles when building Indonesia's future (Sjofjan and Nurfitra 2023). It is noteworthy that in early 2023, a group of Southeast Asian current and former parliamentarians called Indonesia to uphold democratic values and the highest standard of human rights ahead of the 2024 elections (Online Citizen 2023). Such a regional call was made owing to the observation of worsened levels of maintaining democratic, civic and human rights in Indonesia in recent years, deepening the concern that the Indonesian government, upon the elections held in 2024, has to focus on, in part, ameliorating the degree of inclusivity and sustainability of Indonesian society.

Indonesian politicians and policymakers should, therefore, include the discourse on addressing sexual exploitation in the 2024 elections and design concrete, pragmatic and multi-level policies on deconstructing sex trades and disincentivizing disadvantaged women and girls from entering the sex industry. The contents of this book should be topical and valuable as I include a thorough discussion on how multifaceted policies can be formed or amended in order to tackle the ingrained sexual exploitation against socially disadvantaged cohorts. These contents should be taken into consideration by Indonesian and regional policymakers, in the hope that those in authority can be more proactive in response to addressing sexual exploitation against those who are vulnerable, especially when Indonesia recently enacted the anti-extramarital sex law.

The 2024 elections, and, therefore, any political regrouping, will be a suitable timing for established or incoming Indonesian policymakers to change the societal landscape and champion the betterment of socio-economic equality and institutional competitiveness. Here Indonesian policymakers, by tackling the root causes of sexual exploitation, are able to reinforce its regional status not only as the largest democratic country, but also as a nation that materializes its presentation of human rights values.

CONCLUSION

This book uses Indonesia's recent criminalization of extramarital sex to examine how sex work has been constructed and reproduced. Here when extramarital sex is criminalized and morally unjustified and denied, underprivileged cohorts are subject to further vulnerabilities. The problem of sex-related crimes may not attenuate solely because Indonesia has now criminalized any form of extramarital sex. Prostitution, despite being culturally stigmatized and religiously condemned, has been historically common and normalized in Indonesia and Southeast Asia at large. When extramarital sex is criminalized, underprivileged cohorts on the verge of entering, or those who are already working in the sex industry are further marginalized. Passing an extramarital sex criminal code without taking full account of how disadvantaged sex workers would be systematically harmed shows that the Indonesian government would prioritize the national interests (i.e., the fulfilment of socio-cultural and religious obligations as a Muslim-majority country) over the rights of the discriminated, deprived and underprivileged cohorts.

The core concern over Indonesia's extramarital and commercial sex issues is not about whether sexual affairs beyond marital relationships should be allowed. Indonesia should focus on, in addition to the criminalization, not overlooking the importance of empowering those facing poverty and social disadvantages and institutionally reforming the socio-legal, political and law enforcement mechanisms. So long as the chronic, ingrained issues of poverty, socio-economic disadvantages and gender inequality are properly addressed, the prevalence of sex crime shall plausibly attenuate, minimizing the likelihood for Indonesian nationals to seek commercial sex.

As discussed above, eradicating extramarital sex requires the satisfaction of more conditions than that of eliminating commercial sex. This means eliminating commercial sex does not necessarily fully discourage the practice of extramarital sex. However, at the very least, when commercial sex rates are curtailed, the chances of alleviating the performance of extramarital sex shall significantly rise. As a result, by addressing the structural issues in relation to sex work and trafficking, Indonesia can better satisfy its position of criminalizing and deterring extramarital sex.

References

Arimbi, D., G. Putra, and N. Hapsari. 2022. "Sacred Sex or Purely Prostitution? Women's Health during the COVID-19 Pandemic in Roro Kembang Sore Tomb, Tulungaguang, East Java, Indonesia". *Journal of International Women's Studies* 24, no. 8: Article 9. https://vc.bridgew.edu/jiws/vol24/iss8/9

Bah, Y. 2022. "Combating Child Abuse in Indonesia: Achievements and Challenges". *International Journal of Management* 13, no. 3: 192–213.

Bennett, L., and S. Davies. 2015. *Sex and Sexualities in Contemporary Indonesia: Sexual Politics, Health, Diversity and Representations*. London: Routledge.

Black, A., and K. Jung. 2014. "When a Revealed Affair Is a Crime, but a Hidden One Is a Romance: An Overview of Adultery Law in the Republic of Korea". In *The International Survey of Family Law*, edited by B. Atkin, pp. 275–308. Bristol: Jordon Publishing.

Charoensuthipan, P. 2023. "Draft Bill Would Protect, Legalise Sex Work". *Bangkok Post*, 18 March 2023. https://www.bangkokpost.com/thailand/general/2530639/draft-bill-would-protect-legalise-sex-work (accessed 30 March 2023).

Crouch, M. 2009. "Religious Regulations in Indonesia: Failing Vulnerable Groups". *Review of Indonesian and Malaysian Affairs* 43, no. 2: 53–103.

Curley, M. 2014. "Combating Child Sex Tourism in South-east Asia: Law Enforcement Cooperation and Civil Society Partnerships". *Journal of Law and Society* 41, no. 2: 283–314.

Dahles, H. 2009. "Romance and Sex Tourism". In *Tourism in Southeast Asia: New Perspectives*, edited by M. Hitchcock, V. King, and M. Parnwell, pp. 222–35. Honolulu: University of Hawai'i Press.

Davies, S. 2014. "Surveilling Sexuality in Indonesia". In *Sex and Sexualities in Contemporary Indonesia*, edited by L. Bennett and S. Davies, pp. 29–50. London: Routledge.

Dewi, L., and T. Dartanto. 2019. "Natural Disasters and Girls Vulnerability: Is Child Marriage a Coping Strategy of Economic Shocks in Indonesia?". *Vulnerable Children and Youth Studies* 14, no. 1: 24–35.

Franco, G. 2023. "Negotiating the ASEAN Convention Against Trafficking in Persons: Towards a Broader Understanding of Trafficking". In *UN-ASEAN Coordination*, edited by G. Franco, pp. 125–48. Cheltenham: Edward Elgar Publishing.

Fuadi, M., M. Mahbub, I. Dewi, M. Safitry, and S. Sucipto. 2022. "The Historical Study of Prostitution Practices and Its Fiqh Analysis". *Jurnal of Daulat Hukum* 5, no. 2; 92–106.

Hamid, H. 2022. "Sex Traffickers: Friend or Foe?". *Anti-Trafficking Review* 18, no. 1: 87–102.

Hulsbergen, F., and G. Nooteboom. 2022. "Child Sex Tourism: Ambiguous Spaces in Bali". *Tijdschrift voor Economische en Sociale Geografie* 114, no. 1: 28–42.

Hwang, M. 2022. "Differentiated Intimacies: Intimate Labour, Exchange Practices, and Gendered Migration to Hong Kong". *Gender, Place and Culture*, pp. 1–16. https://doi.org/10.1080/0966369X.2022.2146659

Jainah, Z., B. Erlina, I. Seftiniara, M. Safitri, and H. Dunan. 2022. "Strengthening Institutions Recipient of Compulsory Reporting against the Prevalence of Drug Abusers in Lampung Province". *Influence: International Journal of Science Review* 4, no. 2: 316–26.

Mao, F. 2022. "Indonesia Passes Criminal Code Banning Sex Outside Marriage". *BBC News*, 6 December 2022. https://www.bbc.com/news/world-asia-63869078 (accessed 29 March 2023).

Martha, D., K. Setiabudhi, and E. Setyorini. 2022. "Legal Politics Countermeasures of Prostitutions Criminalization Policy Perspective in Indonesia". *Technium Social Sciences Journal* 31, no. 1: 343–48.

Mas'udah, S. 2020. "Resistance of Women Victims of Domestic Violence in Dual-Career Family: A Case from Indonesian Society". *Journal of Family Studies* 28, no. 4: 1580–97.

Muhyidin, M., Y. Adhi, and T. Triyono. 2022. "Contribution of Islamic Law Concerning the Death Penalty to the Renewal of Indonesian Criminal Law". *Indonesian Journal of Advocacy and Legal Services* 4, no. 1: 73–90.

Munro, J. 2023. "West Papuan 'Housewives' with HIV: Gender, Marriage, and Inequality in Indonesia". *Asian Studies Review*. https://doi.org/10.1080/10357823.2023.2188580

Novianti, N., and C. Damayanti. 2022. "International Cooperation to Handle Child Trafficking in Indonesia". *International Journal of Innovative Research and Development* 11, no. 7: 101–7.

Online Citizen, The. 2023. "Southeast Asian Lawmakers Urge Indonesia to Uphold Online Human Rights Ahead of 2024 Elections". 31 May 2023. https://www.theonlinecitizen.com/2023/05/31/southeast-asian-lawmakers-urge-indonesia-to-uphold-online-human-rights-ahead-of-2024-elections/

Pangestu, B., Y. Yuhastina, and A. Rahman. 2022. "The Socio-Cultural Adaption Strategies of Former Commercial Sex Workers in Building the Public Acceptance in RRI Surakarta". *Jurnal Ilmiah Dinamika Sosial* 6, no. 2: 162–74.

Ridho, M., and Y. Nurhayati. 2022. "Comparative Law against Online Prostitution According to Indonesian and Dutch Law". *Jurnal Hukum* 14, no. 1: 231–52.

Ridho, S., and D. Siswantoro. 2023. "Islamic Social Finance, Modern Slavery of Children, and Sustainable Development Goals in Indonesia". *Proceedings of the International Conference on Business and Technology* (ICBT 2021), pp. 729–45.

Saputraa, R., and S. Emovwodo. 2022. "Indonesia as Legal Welfare State: The Policy of Indonesian National Economic Law". *Journal of Human Rights, Culture and Legal System* 2, no. 1: 1–13.

Setiawan, K. 2022. "Vulnerable but Resilient: Indonesia in an Age of Democratic Decline". *Bulletin of Indonesian Economic Studies* 58, no. 3: 273–95.

Shibuya, F., D. Sari, C. Warnaini, A. Rivarti, R. Takeuchi, T. Elizabeth, C. Konneh, C. Reyes, H. Kadriyan, and J. Kobayashi. 2023. "The Process of Overcoming Conflicts among Teachers in the Implementation of Comprehensive Sexuality Education at Ordinary Public Senior High Schools in Mataram City, Indonesia: A Qualitative Study". *Tropical Medicine and Health* 51, no. 7. https://doi.org/10.1186/s41182-023-00495-y

Simorangkir, D., and S. Schumacher. 2022. "Computer-Mediated Social Support for Sexual Harassment Victims: The Case of Sororitas in Indonesia". *Media Asia* 49, no. 4: 288–309.

Sjofjan, F., and T. Nurfitra. 2023. "Komnas HAM Declares Commitment to Human Rights-Friendly Elections". *Antara News,* 11 June 2023. https://en.antaranews.com/news/284775/komnas-ham-declares-commitment-to-human-rights-friendly-elections

Supardin, S., and A. Syatar. 2021. "Adultery Criminalisation Spirit in Islamic Criminal Law: Alternatives in Indonesia's Positive Legal System Reform". *Jurnal Hukum Keluarga dan Hukum Islam* 5, no. 1: 913–27.

Teresia, A., and K. Lamb. 2022. "Indonesia Bans Sex Outside Marriage in New Criminal Code". Reuters, 7 December 2022. https://www.reuters.com/world/asia-pacific/indonesias-parliament-passes-controversial-new-criminal-code-2022-12-06/ (accessed 29 March 2023).

United Nations. N.d.a. "Goal 5: Achieve Gender Equality and Empower All Women and Girls". *Sustainable Development Goals.* https://www.un.org/sustainabledevelopment/gender-equality/ (accessed 22 March 2023).

———. N.d.b. "Promoting Sustained, Inclusive and Sustainable Economic Growth, Full and Productive Employment and Decent Work for All". *Sustainable Development Goals*. https://sdgs.un.org/goals/goal8 (accessed 28 March 2023).

Winarto, H., M. Habiburrahman, F. Kusuma, K. Nuryanto, T. Anggraeni, T. Utami, A. Putra, and D. Syaharutsa. 2023. "Knowledge, Attitude and Practice towards Sexually Transmitted Infections among Women of Reproductive Age in an Urban Community Health Centre in Indonesia". *Open Public Health Journal* 16: e187494452301050. https://doi.org/10.2174/18749445-v16-e230111-2022-182

Epilogue

As of writing this epilogue, I am reading Stiglitz's (2004) *Globalisation and Its Discontents* in my cosy apartment in New Taipei City—on the outskirts of Taipei City, Taiwan. Stiglitz argues the importance of sequencing and timing. The Nobel Prize-winning economist notes one of the major policy mistakes performed by the International Monetary Fund (IMF) and the World Bank in the twentieth century was overlooking the importance of sequencing and timing when applying national and regional policies and interventions. While these national and regional policymaking outputs were supposed to raise the quality of life and national competitiveness of the Global South, very often any improper sequenced policy implementation would counter-discourage developing countries from reaching economic growth and social development.

I am thinking about the importance of sequencing and timing when curbing Indonesia's sex work. It is noteworthy that Indonesia's parliament passed the criminal code against the practice of extramarital sex upon the end of the global public crisis of Coronavirus. While I don't think the timing of passing such a criminal code was intentionally designed (as Indonesia had endeavoured to pass such a code for years), criminalizing extramarital sex soon after the declaration of the end of a pandemic could be beneficial to Indonesia's crackdowns on prostitution and sex trafficking. Owing to the economic downturns caused by the pandemic, Indonesia experienced a budget deficit of 3.0 per cent and 2.4 per cent in 2021 and 2022, respectively. However, upon the end of the public health crisis, the IMF (2023) forecasts that Indonesia will enjoy a 5.0 per cent national economic growth in 2023. These figures presented by the IMF demonstrate that Indonesia is recovering well from the economic downturns and repositions itself on the trajectory to reach more economic success ahead.

Under the climate of positive national economic development, more foreign and domestic investments are plausibly recorded, more job opportunities are created, unemployment rates fall, the availability of public funds that can be used for implementing social protection and pro-poor policies increases, and fewer underprivileged women and children in Indonesia shall experience transitorily or chronically financial hardships. With improved and improving economic climates, the Indonesian government has to take this golden opportunity, upon passing the anti-extramarital sex law, to socio-economically empower more disadvantaged women and children. Such cohorts have to be able to gain access to a fairer share of job, education or vocational training opportunities in order to keep them socially engaged and facilitate their enjoyment of the benefits of human investment.

Institutional reform has to be incorporated into Indonesian policymaking development simultaneously. I already mentioned four times that with the practice of corruption in Indonesia's law enforcement, justice and political mechanisms, more public funds that are supposed to be distributed to underprivileged cohorts are stripped by government officials. the Indonesian government has to champion for a higher degree of transparency and accountability shared among political leaders and law enforcement authorities. Without sufficient transparency and accountability, not only are the efficiency and consistency of the crackdowns on the sex industry hampered, but Indonesia fails to understand clearly how extramarital sex criminalization has progressed. Therefore, heightening the levels of transparency and accountability is the foundation to help Indonesia enhance the desirability and efficiency of its policymaking outputs.

So long as the institutional gaps in curbing sex work are addressed more adequately, Indonesia should tighten its frontline operations, such as applying more regular police raids and online surveillance against any form of cyber-sex crime. As mentioned, with more effective and consistently tightened law enforcement outputs, organized sex crime groups and sex tourists have to assume higher costs if they violate the relevant laws and regulations by expressing criminality. As such, they are discouraged from being involved in sexual transactions, child or adult pornographic production and sex trafficking activities. By then, a shrinking sex trade market can foreseeably be attained in Indonesia.

This book analyses how prostitution is never a stand-alone problem. Prostitution, sex trafficking, poverty, socio-economic inequality, gender inequality, racism, sexism, poor governance, corruption and sex tourism are all interrelated and interdependent within and beyond Indonesian contexts. That is why cracking down on the sex industry is never as simple as criminalizing commercial sex. Indonesia has to strategically and systematically crack down on the underlying unequal power relations by addressing the socio-economic and institutional root causes of prostitution in proper sequencing and timing. So long as the unequal power structure is disrupted and cracked down, Indonesia can, then, realize the development of a more sustainable, liveable and equitable habitat for its population.

References

International Monetary Fund (IMF). 2023. "IMF Staff Completes 2023 Article IV Mission to Indonesia". Press Release No. 23/87. https://www.imf.org/en/News/Articles/2023/03/21/pr2387-indonesia-imf-staff-completes-2023-article-iv-mission-to-indonesia#:~:text=The%20Indonesian%20economy%20has%20weathered,been%20reached%20a%20year%20early (accessed 24 March 2023).

Stiglitz, J. 2004. *Globalisation and Its Discontents*. New York: W.W. Norton & Co.

Index

Jason Hung is a final-year PhD in Sociology candidate at the University of Cambridge. He is a columnist at *The China Global South Project*. He is the author of *Indonesian and Philippine Media on China and COVID-19* (Routledge, 2023); *The Socially Constructed and Reproduced Youth Delinquency in Southeast Asia: Advancing Positive Youth Involvement in Sustainable Futures* (Emerald Publishing, 2023); and *Legalising Prostitution in Thailand: A Policy-Oriented Examination of the (De-)Construction of Commercial Sex* (Springer Nature, 2024).